A JOURNEY INTO
CHINA'S ANTIQUITY

A JOURNEY INTO CHINA'S ANTIQUITY

National Museum of Chinese History

Volume Four

Yuan Dynasty

Ming Dynasty

Qing Dynasty

MORNING GLORY PUBLISHERS

Editor-in-Chief: **Yu Weichao**

Managing Editor: **Xiao Shiling**

Conceived by: **Yan Zhongyi**

Editor: **Zheng Wenlei**

Chinese text by: **Wang Guanzhuo, Chenyu, Liu Ruzhong, Li Zefeng,**

Wang Fang, Su Shengwen, Li Xuemei

Translators: **Gong Lizeng, Yang Aiwen, Xu Keji, Wang Xingzheng**

Photographers: **Yan Zhongyi, Sun Kerang**

Assistant Photographers: **Shao Yulan, Liu Li, Dong Qing**

Maps by: **Zhang Guanying, Zhang Jie, Huang Yucheng, Duan Yong**

Designer: **Zheng Hong**

A JOURNEY INTO CHINA'S ANTIQUITY

Volume Four

Compiled by:

NATIONAL MUSEUM OF CHINESE HISTORY

Published by:

MORNING GLORY PUBLISHERS

35 Chegongzhuang Xilu Beijing 100044 China

Distributed by:

ART MEDIA RESOURCES, LTD.

1507 South Michigan Avenue Chicago IL 60605 USA

Tel: 312-663-5351   Fax: 312-663-5177

First Edition   First Printing 1997

ISBN 7-5054-0514-4/J·0253

37400

Printed in the People's Republic of China

Contents

Yuan Dynasty

(1271—1368)

In the late 13th century, Mongol tribes unified China and established the Yuan Dynasty, ending more than 370 years of political fragmentation that had lasted from the Five Dynasties through the Southern Song. The central, or highest, level of the Yuan Dynasty's administrative structure comprised three branches, the Zhongshu Sheng, in charge of political affairs, Shumi Yuan, military affairs, and Yushi Tai, which handled censorship. Sometimes a separate Shangshu Sheng, or Council of Ministers, was set up but it would not be permanent. The administrative structure at lower levels was varied. Parts of what are now Shandong, Henan and Shanxi provinces and the Inner Mongolia Autonomous Region were called *fuli* (literally "in the belly") and were administered directly by the Zhongshu Sheng. The Tibetan region and fiefs held by princes were under the jurisdiction of the Xuanzheng Yuan, a central organ established to handle religious matters and the civil and military affairs of Tibet. The rest of the country was divided into ten provinces.

Courier stations were built along important land and water routes; great attention was paid to water conservancy; agriculture and handicrafts recovered gradually; priority of development was allotted to certain regions along the country's border; science and technology continued to advance; and foreign trade and cultural exchange with other countries expanded. On the darker side, the Mongolian khans retained some of the outdated systems and practices of Mongol tribes, and many differences existed between the economies of the North and South. Although in their traditional concepts and lifestyles, the various ethnic groups in the country were able to influence each other to some extent, nevertheless there were appreciable differences between them and this conduced to a very uneven development of the economy and culture in different parts of the country, resulting in a complex state of pluralism. Moreover, the policy of ethnic inequality pursued by the khans further aggravated social contradictions.

Rise of Mongolia and Establishment of the Yuan Dynasty

From the 12th to the early 13th century, a number of independent nomadic tribes inhabited the Mongolian plateau. In 1206, the Mongol chieftain Temujin united the various tribes and established the Greater Mongolian State with its capital at Helin (southwest of Ulan Bator in what is now the Mongolian People's Republic). He himself was given the honorific title Genghis Khan. He and his successors continued their military expansion. They subdued the Western Xia in 1227, the Jin in 1234, and the Dali State in 1254; they established ties with the religious leader of Tibet, whereby a basis for governing Tibet was formed; they carried their wars of conquest into Central Asia and Europe. At the height of its power, the Greater Mongolian State included, besides northern China which was directly under central administration, four large khanates whose territory extended over Central Asia and parts of Europe. In 1260 Kublai Khan succeeded to the throne. In 1271 he changed the name of his empire to Yuan, and in the following year moved his capital to Dadu (now Beijing). In 1279 his armies marched south and conquered the Southern Song. By now the Yuan Dynasty had unified the whole of China, including present-day Xinjiang, Yunnan and Tibet.

1. Portrait of Genghis Khan Genghis Khan's (1162-1227) given name was Temüjin. When he established the Mongolian state in 1206, he received the title Genghis Khan, "genghis" being the Mongolian word for "ocean" or "powerful." He organized the Mongolian people into military units using a decimal system based on households rather than individuals. That is, the units were composed of 10, 100, 1,000 or 10,000 households. The commanding generals were members of the nobility. In addition to these units, he formed a regular army of 10,000 men selected from among the scions of the nobility as well as from among ordinary people. This regular army followed the khan into battle in wartime and served as guards in times of peace. Genghis Khan distributed land, slaves and livestock in varying quotas to different ranks of the nobility and promulgated laws and codes to protect their interests. During his lifetime he waged wars of conquest almost unceasingly. He attacked the Jin Dynasty twice, in 1211 and 1215, and captured its capital Zhongdu (Middle Capital, now Beijing). In 1217 he conquered the West Liao. In 1219 he undertook his first expedition to the West, conquering the great Central Asian state of Khwärezm and defeating a joint force of Russians and Kipchaks at the Kalka River in present-day Ukraine. In 1227 he overran the Western Xia but died of illness there the same year.

1

太祖皇帝
即成吉思汗諱帖木真

2. Map of Dadu, capital of the Yuan Dynasty   Dadu was located at the site of what is now Beijing. In 1214, the approach of Mongolian armies forced the Jin Dynasty to move its capital south from Zhongdu (now part of Beijing) to Kaifeng. In the following year, Genghis Khan occupied Zhongdu and restored its original name, Yanjing. But when Kublai Khan succeeded to the throne he changed the name back to Zhongdu and, in 1267, began building a new capital, northeast of the city, called Dadu, or Great Capital. This new capital, completed in 1276, was a rectangular city with a perimeter of 28,600 meters. Its southern wall ran slightly south of what is now the East-West Chang'an Boulevard. Its northern wall is the present "earth city wall" north of Beijing, and its eastern and western walls coincided with the eastern and western city walls built during the Ming and Qing dynasties. There were 11 city gates, of which Heyi Gate and Pingze Gate are the modern Xizhi Gate and Fucheng Gate, and

Map of Dadu, capital of the Yuan Dynasty

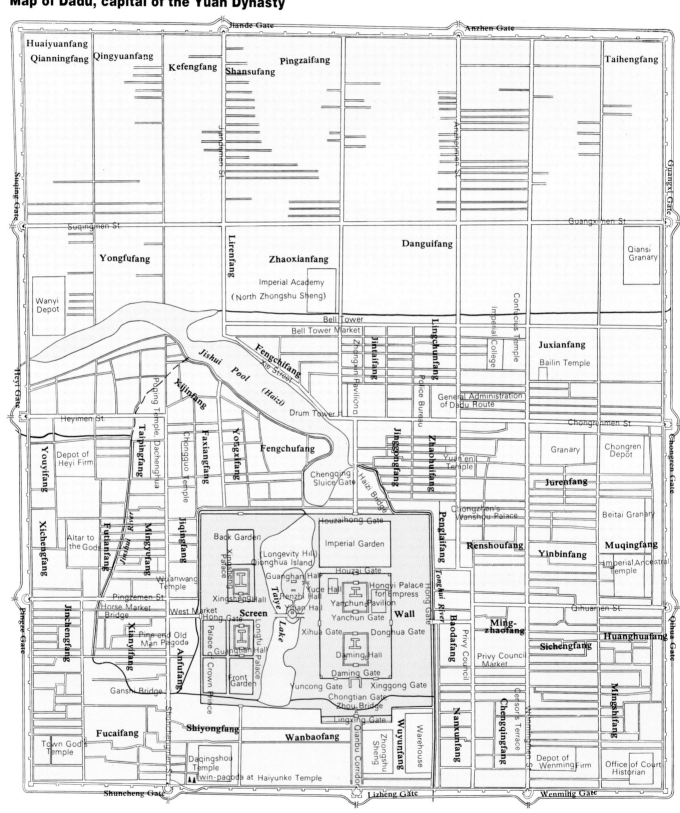

Chongren Gate and Qihua Gate are the modern Dongzhi Gate and Chaoyang Gate. Although all these gates have since been pulled down, their names have been retained as place names in the city. Likewise, Anzhen Gate and Guanxi Gate are now place names in Beijing. The Imperial City was located at the center of southern Dadu, and included the Palace City, Taiye Lake (now the Beihai, Zhonghai and Nanhai lakes) and Wansui Hill (now Qiong Isle in Beihai Park). The main southern entrance to the Imperial City was Lizheng Gate, where Tian'an Men, or the Gate of Heavenly Peace, stands today. The layout of Dadu city was designed according to the principles laid down in the *Book of Rites: Artisan's Record.* Most of the names of the city gates and palace halls also derived from the *Book of Rites.* The streets of Dadu were arranged in an orderly way, running straight from north to south or east to west. In addition, there were many small alleys, called *hutongs,* a term used down to the present.

3. Portrait of Kublai Khan Kublai Khan (1215-1294) was the grandson of Genghis Khan and the first emperor, styled Shizu, of the Yuan Dynasty. In 1251, when still a prince, he was given charge of all civil and military affairs in "Han territory south of the (Gobi) desert," which referred to lands south of Mongolia that were populated by ethnic Han people. In 1253 he conquered Dali state in what is now Yunnan Province, and in the same year received the allegiance of 'Phags-pa, religious leader of Tibet, who presented himself in person to Kublai. In 1260 Kublai succeeded to the

3

throne of the Khanate. In 1271 he changed the dynastic name to Yuan, and in the following year moved his capital to Dadu (now Beijing). In 1279 he conquered the Southern Song and unified the country. As emperor, Kublai Khan advocated "respect for Han laws." He governed the country, enacted laws, established various systems and created

provinces all according to traditional Han patterns. He paid attention to the construction of water conservation projects; laid stress on agriculture and sericulture, regarding them as "urgent tasks"; unified the country's currency system; dredged and widened canals; set up courier stations and developed sea transportation. He strengthened central control over distant border areas and placed Tibet under his direct administration, measures that enhanced the unity of China as a multi-ethnic country.

4. Drip made of yellow-green glazed tile
Yuan structural element; unearthed in 1962 from beneath a Ming Dynasty city wall in the western part of the Beijing Huapi Mill. The front edge of the drip is 22 cm wide; the back, 20 cm. Drips like this were placed along the lower edge of a roof, the tongue pointing downward to facilitate the flow of rainwater. A dragon design, molded in relief on this drip, is glazed in yellow whereas the surrounding space is glazed in green. Evidently, the production of glazed objects was at a fairly advanced stage during the Yuan, for glazed structural members dating from this period have been found in many places in Beijing.

4

5. Carved stone with twin-phoenix, twin-unicorn design   Yuan structural element, 1.2 m long, 1.05 m wide, 0.13 m thick; unearthed from beneath a Ming dynasty city wall in the western part of the Beijing Huapi Mill in 1966. At the center of the upper part of the stone are two phoenixes with their heads turned and wings outspread, carved on a background of intertwining flowers. In the lower part is a pattern of waves and two unicorns.

Additional patterns of intertwining flowers appear on the left and right. Executed proficiently, with lines that flow smoothly and naturally, this is one of the finest examples of stone carving in the Yuan Dynasty. It was probably a slab used to pave the steps of chambers for the empress and imperial concubines in a palace or imperial garden.

6. Seal of 100-Household Crossbow Unit of the Loyal Imperial Bodyguards   Yuan relic, 6.4 cm square, 7 cm in overall height; unearthed in 1956 from under the clay walls of Guangyilong city in the Ulanqab League of the Inner Mongolia Autonomous Region. On the back of this bronze military seal is a square column-like knob. The legend on the seal consists of 11 words in relief in the Mongolian script, which was devised by the Tibetan lama 'Phags-pa. It reads in translation: "Seal of 100-Household Crossbow Unit of

6-1

7-1

6-2

7-2

the Loyal Imperial Bodyguards." On the right side of the knob on the back is the same legend engraved in intaglio in the Han language. On the left side are the legends "Made by the Ministry of Rites, Zhongshu (Political Council)" and "... day of the 5th month of the first year of the Zhizhi reign," both in intaglio and in the Han language. The imperial guards of the Yuan Dynasty were called the Suwei Corps, which garrisoned the capital. The Imperial Bodyguards was a part of the Suwei Corps. The unit was formed in 1292 and its headquarters was called the Imperial Bodyguards Commissioner's Office. This name was temporarily changed to Zhongdu Powerful Guards Commissioner's Office in 1314, but the original name was restored in 1321 and seals were cast for the units under it. Officers of varying ranks commanded units of 1,000 or 100

households. The crossbow unit was a special branch of the Imperial Bodyguards, consisting of 1,000 households divided into ten 100-household units.

7. Seal of Military Department of Wuping County   Yuan relic, 5.8 cm square, 5.1 cm high; unearthed in 1956 in Daming Town, Ningcheng County, Zhaowuda League of the Inner Mongolia Autonomous Region. The legend is in Han seal script and is carved in relief. It consists of six characters that read in translation, "Seal of the Military Department of Wuping County." The same legend, carved in intaglio, appears on the back of the seal. Two other legends, also in intaglio, appear on the back: "Made by the Ministry of Rites, Shangshu Sheng" and "... day, ... month, ... year of the Zhiyuan reign."

During the Yuan Dynasty there was a Zhongshu Sheng at the central level, whose functions resembled those of a secretariat and which handled the nation's political affairs. A Shangshu Sheng (Council of Ministers) was also created now and then and, when it existed, it wielded extensive power. Together with the Zhongshu Sheng, it directed the ministries of civil service, census and revenue, rites, war, criminal justice and public works, and also handled routine political affairs. The seal shown here, cast during the Zhiyuan reign, was probably issued when the first Shangshu Sheng was created. Wuping County (east of the Aohan Banner in what is now the Inner Mongolia Autonomous Region) was under the jurisdiction of the Daning Route of Liaoyang Province in the Yuan Dynasty.

8. Bronze weight of Dadu Route made in the 8th year of the Dade reign   Yuan relic, height 11.1 cm, weight 1.29 kg. The weight has a six-sided body. Carved in intaglio on one side is a legend in Han script that reads in translation: "Made in Dadu Route in the 8th year of the Dade Reign." On another side is the legend "55 catties balance." Dadu Route was the name given to the area around the Yuan capital Dadu. The weight was a part of a standard weighing device made by the authorities of the Dadu Route.

9. *Zhida tongbao, zhizheng tongbao,* coins   Yuan relics, 2.1 cm and 3.4 cm in diameter. Paper money was the principal form of currency used in the Yuan Dynasty, and it was called *jiao chao* or *bao chao.* But the notes were of high

denominations and could not be conveniently used for small purchases. Therefore, some people suggested that coins of smaller value be minted. Such coins were minted only twice during the Yuan, first in 1310, the third year of the reign entitled Zhida. Coins of two denominations were issued, called *dayuan tongbao* and *zhida tongbao.* The second minting was done in 1350, and the coins were called *zhizheng tongbao.* On both occasions, the number of coins minted was insufficient to meet market needs, so the government decreed

9

that "coins minted in previous dynasties can also be used." In Chinese history, it was not unusual for a newly established dynasty to continue using the coins of a previous dynasty — this had happened in all dynasties since the Qin-Han — but it was rare for a government to officially decree that coins of all previous dynasties could be used as legal tender. Some Yuan emperors had so-called "temple coins" minted to be used for donations to Buddhist temples. Such coins were not legal currency, but people also used them as media of exchange.

10. *Zhiyuan tongxing baochao,* paper currency   Yuan relic, 31 cm long, 21.8 cm wide; unearthed in 1959 in the Sagya Temple of the Tibetan Autonomous Region. Two kinds of paper currency were issued in the Yuan Dynasty, called *zhongtong yuanbao jiaochao* and *zhiyuan tongxing baochao.* They were of eleven denominations, from five *wen* to two *guan* (one *wen* was the equivalent of one copper coin, and one *guan* was 1,000 copper coins). The face value of the note shown here is two guan, or 2,000 copper coins. After unifying China, the Yuan rulers strengthened their administration of Tibet, exercising direct control of the region. They established there *xuanwei si* (administrative organs intermediate between provincial and county governments) and *wanhu fu* (organs administering 10,000 households), stationed troops, set up courier stations, levied taxes, circulated currency and carried out censuses. The Sagya sect of Buddhism was dominant in Tibet at the time, and the Sagya Temple was a political and cultural as well as religious center. The discovery there of Yuan paper notes is evidence that the Yuan central government administered Tibet directly.

11. Rafts on Lugou   Yuan silk painting, 143.6 cm high, 105 cm wide. At the center of the painting is an 11-arch bridge. On top of each baluster rests a small stone lion and at the two ends of the bridge are large stone lions, stone elephants and ornamental columns. The bridge resembles the present Lugou Bridge in Beijing, except that its surface is arched whereas the Lugou Bridge slopes very gently. Below the bridge is the Lugou (Lu Ditch), now called the Yongding River. Loads of wood may be seen stacked on both sides of the river; shops line the banks as close together as the teeth of a comb; raftsmen, shop owners, drivers, riders rush around at their work while, in midstream, loaded rafts are borne eastward with the flow. Traffic on this river was busy during the Yuan, and the bridge was where travelers from the south had to cross to reach the capital. The bustling scenes and topographic features depicted in the painting are a truthful representation of what things were like in those days. It is a typical painting of the traditional realistic school, of which unfortunately very few examples are extant.

11-2

Agriculture and Handicrafts

Long years of warfare coupled with the primitive farming methods forced upon the peasants by the Mongolian nobles had seriously disrupted agricultural production in the north and it took some time for production to recover. In some places the peasants organized themselves into "hoe societies," which were like mutual-aid teams to assist each other during the busy seasons. In other places the government used troops or recruited peasants to till government land that had lain waste, thereby increasing the acreage of cultivated farmland. The Yuan rulers also expanded water conservation projects, especially in distant places along the country's border such as Yunnan, Gansu and Ningxia, where dams, dikes and other installations that had been damaged were repaired and restored to use. In the wake of these achievements, several important works on agriculture appeared, among them the *Book of Agriculture* and *Essentials of Agriculture and Sericulture.* Some progress was also made in handicrafts. In villages south of the Yangtze, where spinning and weaving machines had been greatly improved, cotton spinning and weaving began to play an important role in household handicrafts. Techniques for making porcelain and applying glaze all advanced to higher levels. Porcelain objects in blue and red underglaze occupy important places in the history of Chinese ceramics. Notable achievements were also made in silk weaving, jade carving and the manufacture of articles of gold, silver and lacquer.

12. *Book of Agriculture*, compiled by Wang Zhen Movable type edition printed in Qing emperor Qianlong's time. Wang Zhen was a famous agronomist in the Yuan Dynasty. In the first year (1295) of the Yuanzhen reign, he was appointed magistrate of Jingde County (in present-day Anhui Province). He began compiling the *Book of Agriculture during* his tenure there and, at the same time, developed the technique of printing with movable wooden type, which he used to print 100 volumes of *Local Records of Jingde County.* In 1300, he was transferred to the magistracy of Yongfeng County (in present-day Jiangxi Province) where he completed in two years' time the initial draft of his book on agriculture. It was published from engraved blocks in 1313. Twenty-two volumes of the book are extant, and these may be divided into three major parts: "Rhymed Formulas for Agriculture and Sericulture" (Vols. 1-6), "Catalogue of a Hundred Crops" (Vols. 7-10) and "Illustrated Catalogue of Farm Machinery and Tools" (Vols. 11-22). The first part deals with the history of the development of agriculture and techniques used and experiences gained in farming, forestry, animal husbandry, side-occupations and fisheries. The second part shows how to plant and cultivate various crops, including vegetables, fruits, trees and bamboo. The third part describes machines and tools used in farming, cotton spinning and weaving and silk weaving and includes 306 illustrations. An appendix systematically explains the techniques for making, storing, indexing and printing with movable wooden type. This book is a summary of farm technology up to and including the Yuan period.

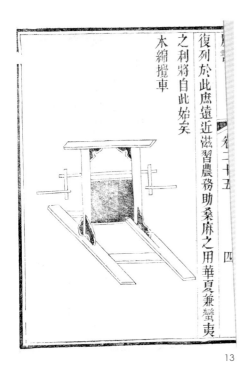

木綿攪車

復列於此庶遠近滋習農務助桑麻之用華夏兼蠻夷

之利寧自此始矣

卷二十五

四

13

13. Cotton gin Illustration from Wang Zhen's *Book of Agriculture*. This was a machine for removing seeds from raw cotton fiber — a cotton gin. There were two cylinders in the machine, operated by hand and rotated in opposite directions. Cotton was fed into the space between the cylinders. The seeds were squeezed out and dropped inside the machine while the clean cotton fibers fell through to the outside. Although its structure was simple, the machine was able to raise productivity enormously by utilizing the principle of applying pressure through reverse revolving cylinders and using leverage.

14. Spinning wheel Illustration from Wang Zhen's *Book of Agriculture*. This was a machine for spinning yarn or thread. The large wheel was moved by a foot-pedal and, by means of a cord, caused three spindles to rotate. The spinner held a roll of cotton fibers and, coordinating with the movement of the spindles, drew out a length of fiber from the roll. When this had been twisted to a certain extent the spinner would wind the

new thread on a spindle. This process of drawing out fibers, twisting and winding them was then repeated to make more thread. Using both the hands and the feet, the spinner could spin three lengths of fiber at one time.

15. Textile cradle Illustration from Wang Zhen's *Book of Agriculture*. Before the Yuan Dynasty, newly spun yarn had to be unwound from the spindle and rewound on a framelike machine called *boche* (literally "adjusting machine"), from which it was removed in bundles before being starched in preparation for the next step in the work process. As only one length of yarn or thread could be wound on a *boche* at a time, the efficiency was low. In the early Yuan, a new machine called *renchuang* (literally "textile cradle") was invented and tested in places in what is now Fujian Province. Its function was similar to that of a *boche;* it was also a machine for winding yarn, but it could wind eight strands of yarn and form them into bundles at the same time, thus greatly increasing speed and efficiency.

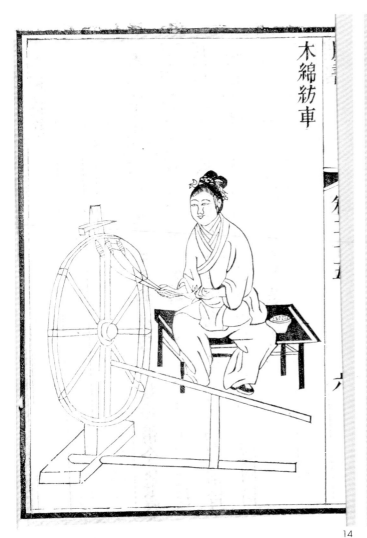

木綿紡車

木綿軖牀

14

15

17

16. Pear-shaped vase with flared lip and blue-and-white cloud-dragon design
Yuan ornamental object, height 29.8 cm, mouth diameter 8.4 cm, base diameter 9.9 cm. This is a vase with underglaze coloring, a technique in which two layers of glaze must be applied to the biscuit: a layer of colored glaze under a layer of transparent glaze. As each layer must be fired separately, two successive firings are needed. If cobalt is added to the first layer, the finished product has a blue color and is popularly called blue-and-white porcelain. Differences in the cobalt content and in kiln temperature created different shades of blue. This technique was already known during the Tang and Song periods, but was not widely used. It was not until the Yuan that blue-and-white porcelain wares were produced in large quantity. Pear-shaped vases with flared lips like the one shown here also appeared in earlier periods and they continued to be popular during the Yuan. The Yuan vases, however, had shorter necks and more rounded bellies. The ring base was very low, so low that the bottom of the vase appeared to be flat, thus enhancing the steadiness of the object.

17. Blue-and-white porcelain wine vessel with plantain leaf pattern   Yuan ornamental object, height 16 cm, mouth diameter 7.5 cm, base diameter 6 cm; unearthed in 1980 from a Yuan Dynasty cellar in Gao'an County, Jiangxi Province. Vessels of this kind, called *gu* in Chinese, were originally made to hold wine. Over time they lost their practical value and became ritual vessels. The *gu* shown here was modeled after an antique and was made for display only.

18. Pear-shaped vase with flared lip and pattern of intertwining chrysanthemum in underglaze red Yuan ornamental object, height 32.1 cm, mouth diameter 8.4 cm, belly diameter 20.1 cm, base diameter 12.2 cm. There are two layers of glaze, a colored layer below and a transparent one above, which were fired at the same time. The colored glaze contained copper and assumed a red color after firing; hence it is called underglaze red. The technique was an invention of the Yuan Dynasty. The vase shown here is only light red in color, as the technique of mixing glaze ingredients and controling furnace temperature was not yet fully developed at the time.

19-1

19-2

19. Large bowl with intertwining peony in underglaze red Yuan relic, height 16.2 cm, mouth diameter 41.8 cm, base diameter 22.8 cm. This is the largest underglaze red bowl so far discovered among Yuan Dynasty porcelain.

20-1

20. Porcelain plate of Shufu Kiln Yuan relic, height 4.3 cm, mouth diameter 13.3 cm, base diameter 4.5 cm. A product of the Shufu Kiln in Jingdezhen, it was made on the order of the Shufu Yuan, an advisory body of the Yuan court. Impressed under the glaze on the ring base are the Chinese characters for *shufu*. Most of the objects fired in the Shufu Kiln were plates, bowls and small basins for washing writing brushes, and all were somewhat thick and heavy. The most common designs were intertwining flowers and double dragons, which were impressed from molds. The glaze was white with a tinge of blue and was sometimes called egg-white glaze.

20-2

21

21. Vase with intertwining peony, product of Longquan Kiln Yuan relic, height 45.5 cm, mouth diameter 19.5 cm, base diameter 13 cm; unearthed in 1970 at the site of Fengzhou city of the Yuan Dynasty, east of Huhhot in the Inner Mongolia Autonomous Region. Longquan (Dragon Spring) Kiln was located in present-day Longquan County, Zhejiang Province. It began operation in the Northern Song and continued to produce ceramics down to the Yuan. Its products belonged to the category of celadons. Because of the presence of ferrous oxide in the glaze, the objects assumed various shades of blue after firing, depending on the amount of iron content. Some were earthy yellow or brown, but the most common colors were pale blue and light green. Many objects had distinctive shapes such as cups with long stems, vases with narrow necks or ringlike ears, jars with lotus-shaped covers. In addition to the carved and embossed designs popular during the Song period, Yuan craftsmen also decorated their objects with impressed designs, pasted designs and openwork. The neck of the vase shown here is decorated with a cord pattern. On the upper part of the belly is a carved intertwining peony design, and on the lower part a pattern of lotus petals in relief. The entire vessel is glazed in a smooth and lustrous light blue. It is one of the best examples of Longquan ceramics.

22. White-glazed porcelain jar with black design of children at play, product of Cizhou Kiln Yuan container, height 30 cm, mouth diameter 18.5 cm, belly diameter 31 cm, base diameter 12 cm; discovered in 1994 near a sunken ship of the Yuan Dynasty off the coast of Sandaogang, Suizhong County, Liaoning Province. The kilns of Cizhou were built on the banks of the Zhang River in Ci County, Hebei Province. They produced mostly jars, plates, bowls and vases, and occasionally porcelain pillows and small toys. The glaze was white with a tinge of yellow, and the decorations were painted or carved in black or brown. The most common designs were of children at play, fishing, dragons, phoenixes, ripples, and curled leaves and flowers. Executed simply and vigorously, they are full of folk charm. This jar of sturdy build has a design of children painted with black glaze on a white-glazed background, a typical feature of Cizhou ceramics.

22-1

23. Vase with openwork stand, product of Jun Kiln Yuan ornamental object, height 58.3 cm, mouth diameter 17 cm, base diameter 18 cm; unearthed in 1970 at the site of Fengzhou city of the Yuan dynasty, east of Huhhot, Inner Mongolia Autonomous Region. The Jun Kiln was located in what is now Yu County, Henan Province. Its products belong to the category of northern celadons, whose glaze is basically blue-green but varies greatly in shade. Unlike other kinds of celadon, the finished products of the Jun Kiln have a milky rather than a glassy appearance, due to the relatively thick glaze coating. Porcelain objects of the Yuan Dynasty fired in the Jun Kiln were mostly vases, plates, bowls, basins and wine vessels; there were also some antique replicas. The vase shown here was glazed in sky blue all over, but the glaze was not applied evenly. As it was spread too thickly, some of it flowed to the bottom during firing, a phenomenon popularly called "flowing glaze." There are large specks of red on the vase, caused by the reduction of the copper content during firing.

24

24. Pear-shaped vase with flared lip and carved floral design in blue-white glaze
Yuan ornamental object, height 29 cm, base diameter 9.4 cm; unearthed in Jinan, Shandong Province, in 1956. The glaze used on this vase contained a small amount of ferrous oxide, which caused the whiteness of the glaze to be permeated with a bluish green after firing. Glaze of this color that is neither blue nor white but resembles both blue and white is called "blue-white" or "shadowy blue" glaze. The finest porcelain objects of this kind are those fired in the kilns of Jingdezhen in Jiangxi Province.

25

25. Silver pear-shaped vase with flared lip Yuan relic, height 51.5 cm, mouth diameter 9.5 cm, belly diameter 23.5 cm, base diameter 12 cm; unearthed in Hefei, Anhui Province, in 1955. It has a plain surface with no decoration and is an imitation of a porcelain vase. Inscribed on the bottom of other silver vessels unearthed in the same place and at the same time are legends that say this collection of silverware was made by a smith known as Zhang Zhongying in the Ding Family Shop in Luzhou (now Hefei, Anhui Province) in 1333, the fourth year of the Zhishun reign of the Yuan Dynasty.

Domestic and Overseas Trade and Transportation

Southeastern China was the chief source of tax revenues in the Yuan Dynasty. To ensure that grain and other supplies from this part of the country could be delivered continuously to Dadu (now Beijing) in the north, the Yuan government built three new waterways and rebuilt the Sui-Tang Grand Canal so that it followed a straighter course and reached the interior of Dadu. Additionally, it opened a sea-lane from the mouth of the Yangtze River to Dagukou on the Bo Sea. With faster and easier transportation between north and south, the country's domestic trade flourished as never before. Besides Dadu, a number of other cities such as Hangzhou, Chengdu, Yangzhou, Suzhou and Fuzhou also became prosperous commercial centers, and overseas trade also developed. Among the principal ports opened to foreign trade were Quanzhou, Guangzhou and Qingyuan (now Ningbo, Zhejiang Province). Foreign envoys, merchants, scientists and missionaries came to China in large numbers and many took up permanent residence here.

26. Map of sea transportation and canals of the Yuan Dynasty   Each year the Yuan imperial court had to bring in large quantities of grain and other supplies to Dadu from the southeast. The old Sui-Tang Grand Canal that centered on Luoyang (in Henan Province) not only followed a winding course but had inadequate sources of water. Therefore, Emperor Shizu of Yuan ordered the building of two new canals, called Jizhou and Huitong, in Shandong Province and a third canal called Tonghui linking Tongzhou (now Tongxian, Beijing) with Dadu. It took nearly ten years (1283-1292) to build these new waterways, but when completed they formed — together with the section of the old canal that passed through Hebei, Jiangsu and Zhejiang provinces — a relatively straight course to Dadu and grain for the capital began to flow in via this new route. This canal still exists and is called the Beijing-Hangzhou Grand Canal. At about the same time, the Yuan rulers tried shipping supplies by sea from the mouth of the Yangtze northward to Zhigu (now Tianjin). By 1293, the sea route had replaced the canal as the principal means of transportation.

Map of sea transportation and canals of the Yuan Dynasty

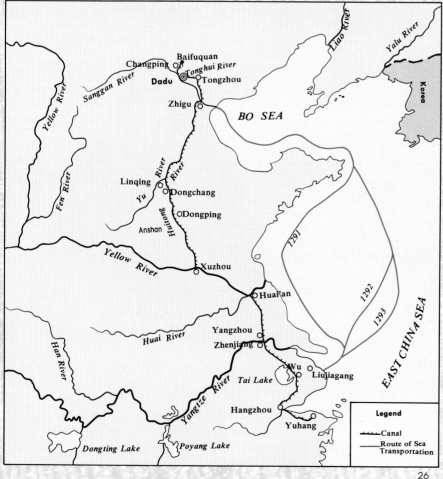

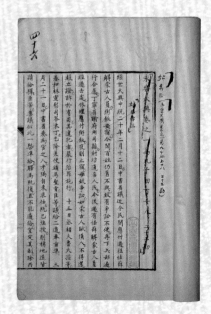

Map showing transport routes between China and other countries during the Yuan Dynasty

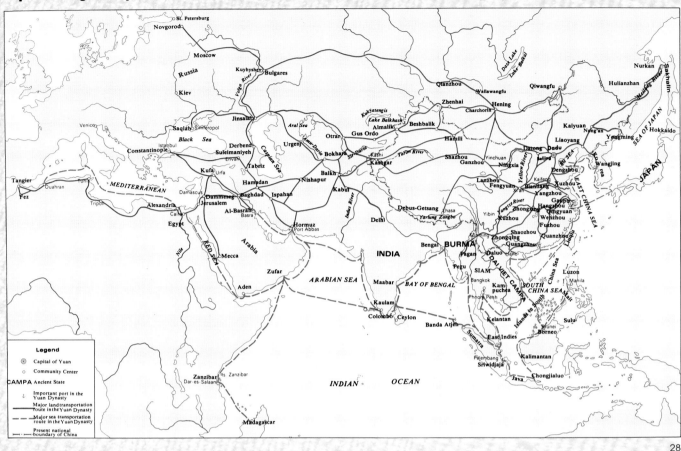

28

27. *Yongle Encyclopedia: Courier Stations,* private hand-copied version

The *Yongle Encyclopedia,* completed during the Yongle reign of the Ming Dynasty, contained detailed accounts of the courier system of the Yuan. In ancient China, many courier stations were built along major transportation routes, forming a nationwide network that offered temporary abodes for traveling officials and couriers, and also served as places to change their means of transportation if necessary. This network was expanded and streamlined during the Yuan Dynasty, and at one time had as many as 1,519 stations. The areas they covered extended to Nurkan (at the mouth of the Heilong River) in the northeast, to Kirgiz (in the upper reaches of the Yenisey River) in the north, and to the Tibetan region in the southwest.

28. Map showing transport routes between China and other countries during the Yuan Dynasty
Thanks to the improved techniques of shipbuilding and navigation developed during the Song Dynasty, overseas trade and communications were able to make enormous progress during the Yuan. The Yuan government set up special entities to handle foreign trade. These entities, collectively called the Office of Municipal Shipping, which functioned like today's customs offices, were originally located at seven places. Later, through adjustment and merging, only three offices remained, the ones at Quanzhou, Guangzhou and Qingyuan. The Quanzhou office became the largest port in the country at a time when China had trade relations with more than 100 countries and regions. Its overseas trade reached Japan and Korea to the east and the eastern shores of Africa to the west. Its principal exports were still porcelain and silk goods, but its imports numbered over a hundred kinds of goods, including spices, medicine, ivory, exotic rarities and timber.

29. *Local Customs of Zhenla* by Zhou Daguan
Zhou Daguan was a native of Yongjia County (now Wenzhou, Zhejiang Province) in the Wenzhou Route of the Yuan Dynasty. In 1295 (the first year of the Yuanzhen reign) he paid a visit to Zhenla (present Cambodia) as a member of a diplomatic mission, voyaging by boat from Wenzhou port. After returning to China in 1297, he compiled what he had seen and heard into a book that describes under 40 headings the cities, palaces, royal tours, armed forces, officialdom, language, clothing, products, geography, animals and plants, means of transportation, trade, customs and lifestyles of Zhenla. It was the one and only history of Zhenla at the time. It also mentions the navigational routes of Chinese shipping and records such details as the points of the compass during sea voyages.

29

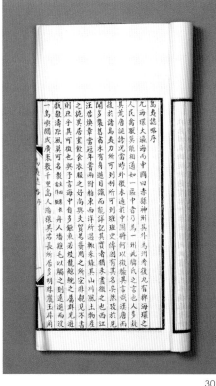

30

China's Penghu and Taiwan Province. The 100th entry, subtitled "A Collection of the Strange and Unusual," contains abstracts from the works of earlier writers. The remaining 97 entries describe the customs, beliefs, products and tradable goods of various countries and regions. Altogether over 220 places and 347 items of tradable goods are mentioned. Most of the goods were among China's import needs; some were China's exports. As the contents were largely based on the author's personal experiences, they are specific and invaluable as reference material for the study of overseas trade and transportation during the Yuan.

31. Porcelain bowls of Longquan Kiln
Food containers of Yuan, mouth diameters 15.7 to 17 cm; recovered in 1969 from a sunken ship of the Yuan Dynasty found off the coast of Wenzhou Island, Zhuhai, Guangdong Province. All three bowls were

fired at Longquan Kiln. As the ferrous oxide content of the glaze exceeded 5%, the blue color of the glaze darkened into shades of brown after firing. Porcelain articles were among the principal exports of the Yuan. The bowls were part of a large cargo of porcelain carried by the ship, which sank near Wenzhou Island after leaving Guangzhou harbor.

32. Records of diplomatic missions to Persia inscribed on stone Yuan relic, 67 cm wide, 27 cm high; unearthed in the southern outskirts of Quanzhou, Fujian Province, in 1953. The original tablet is in the Quanzhou Museum of the History of Overseas Transportation. The inscription says the writer had brought a tribute of precious articles from Persia to the Great Yuan and was graciously received by the Yuan emperor. Subsequently, in the third year (1299) of the Dade reign, he was sent as an envoy to Persia, carrying with him a

30. *Records of Exotic Islands* by Wang Dayuan Wang Dayuan was a native of Nanchang Prefecture (now Nanchang city, Jiangxi Province). Towards the end of the Yuan Dynasty (c.1330-1339) he undertook two sea voyages aboard trade ships, visiting many places. Wherever he stopped, he would note down the topography and climate of the place, its products, and the customs and lifestyles of its people. Upon his return he compiled what he had seen and heard into a book entitled *Records of Exotic Islands,* the contents of which are listed under 100 entries. In the first and second entries, subtitled "Penghu" and "Liuqiu (today's Taiwan)," he introduced conditions in

31

32

33-1

plaque inscribed with gold characters. He was received by the Persian king, Mahmud Ghazan, who presented him with seven precious gifts. On his return, he showed these to the Yuan court, where he was again treated courteously. Later he returned to his native Quanzhou and died in the eighth year (1304) of the Dade reign. As some details are missing at the beginning and end of the inscription, it is obvious that the original records were inscribed on more than one tablet, of which only the one shown here has been found. The writer may have been a merchant from Quanzhou who while on a visit to Persia was asked by the Persian king to bring a tribute to the Yuan court. Because of this he found favor with the Yuan emperor and was sent as an envoy to Persia. This is an example of how merchants engaged in overseas trade were used as interim couriers to other countries during the Yuan Dynasty.

28	4	3	31	35	10
36	18	21	24	11	1
7	23	12	17	22	30
8	13	26	19	16	29
5	20	15	14	25	32
27	33	34	6	2	9

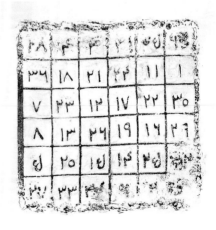

33-2

33. Square iron board with Arabic numerals Yuan relic, 14.2 cm square; unearthed in 1956 at the site of the palace of the prince of Anxi of the Yuan Dynasty, in Xi'an, Shaanxi Province. On this iron board is a large square divided into 36 small squares (6 x 6), in each of which is a number, from 1 to 36 but not in numerical order. The numbers in each row, column or diagonal all add up to 111. This is a compound magic square, for within the large square is a smaller one, 4 x 4, in which the numbers in each row, column or diagonal all add up to 74. Magic squares originated in Arabia and were introduced into China during the Yuan.

Science and Culture

There were two distinctive features in the science and culture of the Yuan Dynasty. First, their development was a continuation of the development of the science and culture of the preceding Song Dynasty. Second, because of greater unity in the country and its expanded foreign relations, Yuan science and culture were pluralistic in nature, the merging of different schools. Yuan astronomy and mathematics were among the most advanced in the world. Notable progress was also made in medicine, shipbuilding, porcelain making and textiles. In culture, Yuan *qu*, a type of verse for singing, became the newest and most important form of literature. Painting and calligraphy also reached new heights and many excellent works of Yuan artists have survived down to the present.

34. Abridged armilla Ming relic, 4.7 m long, 3.25 m wide, 3.1 m high; the original is in the Purple Mountain Observatory in Nanjing, Jiangsu Province. The first abridged armilla was made by Guo Shoujing (1231-1316), an eminent scientist of the Yuan Dynasty and a native of Xingtai (in present Hebei Province) of the Shunde Route. An expert in astronomy and water conservation, he was the chief engineer in the building of the north-south Grand Canal and in many other water conservancy projects. He also supervised the transport of grain along the Tonghui Canal. In astronomy, he is credited with the setting up of 27 stations for large-scale observation of celestial phenomena during the early years of the Yuan. He compiled the Time-Service Calendar, the most accurate calendar in the world at the time. It divided a year into 365.2425 days, which differed by only 26 seconds from the real time for the earth to complete a revolution around the sun. He was also adept at making instruments. He invented or improved upon 13 astronomical instruments, including the abridged armilla. Because of his historic role in the development of astronomy, later generations named a lunar crater "Gou Shoujing" in his honor. Gou Shoujing simplified the structure of a traditional armillary sphere used in China, reducing the number of layers so that it could be used more easily. It was therefore called the abridged armilla, and consisted of three parts. The upper part was an equatorial theodolite (with a sighting-tube ring, an equatorial circle and a centigrade circle) used to observe the equatorial coordinates of celestial bodies. On the northern side of the lower part was an altazimuth (with horizontal and vertical circles) to measure the azimuth and altitude of a celestial body. On the southern side was a calibrator to check

34

and adjust the north-south direction of the instrument. To ensure that the centigrade and equatorial circles could revolve freely, a ball bearing, the first in the world, was placed between them. The abridged armilla shown here, now residing in the Purple Mountain Observatory, was made between 1437 and 1442, during the Zhengtong reign of the Ming Dynasty. It is an exact imitation of Gou Shoujing's instrument, except that a sundial has been added in the part which contains the calibrator.

35. Bronze tank water clock Device for measuring time made in 1316, the third year of the Yanyou reign of the Yuan Dynasty. It consisted of four tanks — the sun tank, moon tank, star tank and water receiving tank. The sun tank was 75.5 cm tall, 68.2 cm in diameter at the top and 60 cm at the base; the moon tank 58.5 cm tall, 54.5 cm in diameter at the top and 53 cm at the base; the star tank 55.4 cm tall, 44 cm in diameter at the top and 39 cm at the base; and the water receptacle 75 cm tall, 32 cm in diameter at the top and 31 cm at the base. The four tanks were placed in the given order at stair-step levels on a stand. Their overall height from the top of the sun tank to the bottom of the stand was 264.4 cm. Water trickled at a uniform speed from the sun tank to the moon tank, to the star tank, and finally into the water receptacle. At the center of the lid of the water receptacle was a bronze scale graduated according to the hours of the day. In front of the scale was a wooden pointer whose lower end was affixed to a wooden block called a pontoon inside the receptacle. As the water in the receptacle accumulated, the pontoon and pointer rose slowly. The mark indicated by the pointer at any given instant showed the time of day. The earliest water clocks had only one tank. Devices with multiple tanks were invented later. The one shown here is the earliest extant example of a multiple tank water clock.

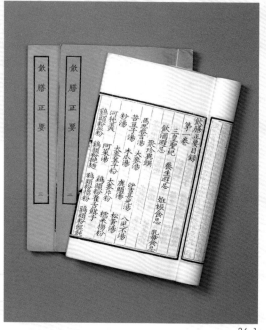

36-1

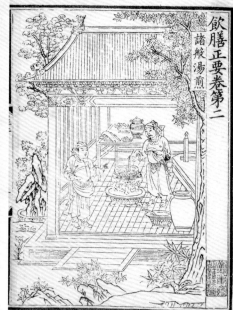

36-2

36. *Essentials of Dietetics* by Huosihui Huosihui was a Mongol who once served as dietitian in the Yuan imperial court. Well versed in dietetics, he supervised the preparing of palace meals. This book, in three volumes with 168 illustrations, is an important ancient work on nutrition and food therapy. It discusses a wide range of dietary problems, e.g. what foods should be avoided from a nutritional point of view, what should be avoided when drinking alcohols or taking medicine, the diets for pregnant women and wet nurses, exotic foods and rarities, variations of the five flavors, diseases that require food therapy, the beneficial and harmful effects of foods, foods with opposite effects, food poisoning, etc. It analyzes the nutritive values of foods commonly consumed by Mongolians, Han, Hui, Tibetan and other nationalities, describes their cooking techniques, and shows how to regulate one's diet and what substances to avoid.

38. Illustration of revolving wheel typesetter Bi Sheng of the Northern Song, who invented movable clay type, also experimented with printing from wooden type but the results were not satisfactory and he gave up. Later, in the early years of the Yuan, Wang Zhen, an agronomist, tried printing from movable wooden type and in the process invented a typesetter with a revolving wheel. He

was the magistrate of Jingde (in present Anhui Province) at the time. Over a period of two years, he had 30,000 pieces of wooden type made, with which he printed 100 volumes of *Records of Jingde County* in less than a month's time. The revolving wheel typesetter facilitated both the location of characters and the setting of type. The wheel was divided into a number of compartments, in which the wooden type was arranged in groups of characters that rhymed. It was affixed on a vertical axis and could be turned. When in use, one person would read the text and a second person would turn the wheel, pick out the corresponding pieces of type and place them in a printing bed. After the text had been printed, the pieces would be replaced on the wheel in the same order.

37. Ancient Uygur movable wooden type Yuan printing implements, 2.3 cm long, 1 cm wide, 0.5-1.4 cm thick; discovered in the Mogao Caves of Dunhuang County, Gansu Province, in 1908. Printing from movable type had been introduced into northwestern China by the Yuan Dynasty. As the Uygur language was used in the region, wooden type with ancient Uygur script was carved there. The types differed in thickness because the letters of ancient Uygur differed in size.

37

39-2

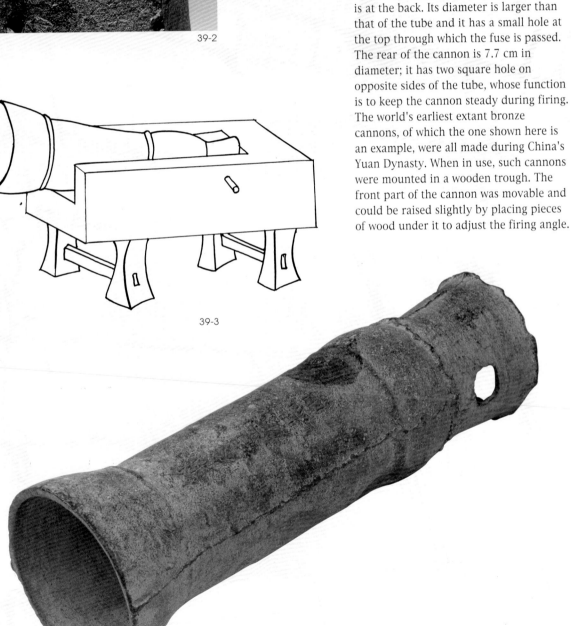

39-3

39-1

39. Illustration of bronze cannon Tube-shaped weapon for firing projectiles; discovered in 1935 in Yunju Temple, Fangshan County (now part of Beijing), Hebei Province. It was cast in 1332, the third year of the Zhishun reign of the Yuan Dynasty, weighs 6.94 kg, is 35.3 cm long, and has a flared muzzle 10.5 cm in diameter. The diameter of the tube is a little smaller; and when in use, it was filled with pellets and other objects. Carved lengthwise in intaglio on the outer wall of the tube is the legend, "14th day of the 2nd month of the 3rd year of Zhishun's reign. Army for keeping peace and suppressing bandits on the border, No. 300, Mashan." The powder magazine is at the back. Its diameter is larger than that of the tube and it has a small hole at the top through which the fuse is passed. The rear of the cannon is 7.7 cm in diameter; it has two square hole on opposite sides of the tube, whose function is to keep the cannon steady during firing. The world's earliest extant bronze cannons, of which the one shown here is an example, were all made during China's Yuan Dynasty. When in use, such cannons were mounted in a wooden trough. The front part of the cannon was movable and could be raised slightly by placing pieces of wood under it to adjust the firing angle.

40-1

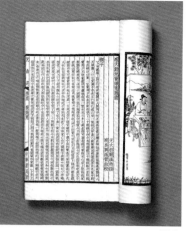

40-2

40. Script of *The Injustice to Dou E*, poetic drama by Guan Hanqing   Guan Hanqing, native of Dadu (now Beijing), was a great dramatist of the Yuan Dynasty, born in the final years of the Jin (Nuzhen) Dynasty. He died during the Dade reign (1297-1307) of the Yuan. He wrote more than 60 poetic dramas, among which the complete scripts of 13 are extant. The most famous are *The Injustice to Dou E, Rescued by a Coquette, Pavilion for Worshipping the Moon* and *Riverside Pavilion*. He also left behind 14 collections of miscellaneous songs and 52 shorter verses. Most of his works praise heroes and true lovers, expose the dark side of society and attack corrupt officials and local tyrants. They reveal the sufferings of the oppressed and extol their defiant spirit. The language is simple but beautiful, and the dramatic characters are clearly defined. *The Injustice to Dou E* is the story of a widow, Dou E, who was maltreated by a man called Zhang Lu'er, and who was wrongly accused of murder and sentenced to death. Just before her execution, she pointed to heaven and made three vows. After her death, to everybody's astonishment, the three vows all came true. In the end, her father, who had become an official, was able to redeem her name. This drama is regarded as one of the four great tragedies of Chinese classical drama.

41. Script of *The West Chamber*, poetic drama by Wang Shifu   Wang Shifu, native of Dadu (now Beijing), was a great dramatist of the Yuan Dynasty and the noted author of 14 dramas. The most famous is *The West Chamber*, based on an earlier work called *Palace Songs of the West Chamber* by Dong Xieyuan of the

Jin (Nuzhen) Dynasty. It tells the story of the love between Zhang Sheng, a young scholar, and Cui Yingying, a young woman in the prime minister's household. Their attachment to each other in the face of overwhelming odds reflects the younger generation's opposition to feudal rites. This drama broke away in form from the four-act pattern of Yuan poetic dramas. Consisting of 21 acts, it was a drama of unusual length in its time.

42. Mural painting of Actor Zhongdu Xiu of the Taihang Mountains   Yuan painting, 390 x 312 cm; the original is in Prince Mingying's Hall, Guangsheng Temple, Hongdong County, Shanxi Province. Executed in 1324, the first year of Yuan emperor Taiding's reign, it depicts a scene from a Yuan poetic drama. Inscribed horizontally on the painting is a legend that reads in translation: "Actor Zhongdu Xiu of the Taihang Mountains performed here." Yuan dramas were of two major categories, poetic dramas and southern dramas. Poetic dramas developed faster and had a greater impact on later works. They were performed mostly in the north, in the provinces of Shanxi and Hebei in the beginning, and consisted primarily of singing, but also included some *ke* (acting) and *bai* (dialogue), special terms that are still used in operas today. In the painting, the figure in the center wearing a headdress and long robe and holding a tablet is Zhongdu Xiu. "Xiu" was a suffix used after the names of all leading actors in Yuan Dynasty poetic dramas.

43-1

43. Clay figurines playing the flute and striking clappers Yuan funerary objects, height of figurines 38.5 and 36.5 cm respectively; unearthed in 1965 from a Yuan tomb in Fengfeng village, west of Jiaozuo city, Henan Province. Dramas known as *zaju* were performed in the Liao, Song and Jin dynasties but the methods of performance varied during different historic periods. *Zaju* of the Yuan Dynasty, also called *Yuanqu* and sometimes translated as poetic drama, was a new form of opera. It generally consisted of four acts, with a prologue added when necessary. The roles in the opera were called *zhengmo* (middle-aged male lead), zhengdan (leading female), *jing* (painted-face role, usually a person of rough character) and *fujing* (secondary *jing* role). In general, the *zhengmo* and *zhengdan* were the lead singers; the others played supporting roles. The melody in any act was composed of tunes that followed the same pattern. There were many famous *zaju* writers during the Yuan Dynasty, and more than 160 *zaju* operas from this period have survived down to the present. The two figurines shown here, one playing a flute, the other striking clappers, represent a part of the orchestral accompaniment to a *zaju* performance.

老懷語

小令酌郭

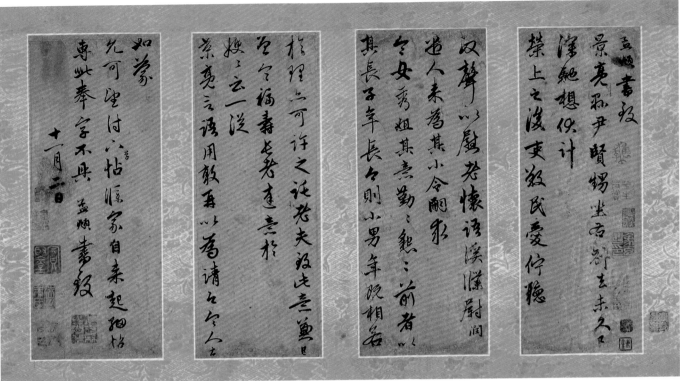

44. Zhao Mengfu's letter to Jing Liang Letter on four sheets, each 29 x 11.5 cm. Zhao Mengfu (1254-1322), styled Zi'ang, nicknamed the Pine-and-Snow Taoist, was a native of Huzhou (in present Zhejiang Province) and a scion of the Song royal family. During the early Yuan, he received through recommendation a post as an official in the imperial court where he gradually advanced, eventually becoming the head of all scholars of the Imperial Academy. He was an accomplished calligrapher, painter, poet, prose writer and musician. He could write well in various scripts, including seal, official, regular, running and cursive and, by assimilating the best of different schools, formed his own Zhao-style. In painting, he excelled in landscapes, rock-and-bamboo, figures, horses and riders, flowers and birds, many of which are considered to be timeless works of art. No other artist of the Yuan Dynasty has left to later generations so many fine paintings and calligraphic pieces as Zhao Mengfu.

45. *Hills and Water in the Rain* by Huang Gongwang Yuan painting, 217.5 x 30 cm. Painting attained a very high artistic level during the Yuan Dynasty. The most representative works of this period were the landscapes and impressionist paintings done by men of letters, among whom the most famous names are Zhao Mengfu, Qian Xian, Gao Kegong, Huang Gongwang, Wang Meng, Wu Zhen and Ni Zan. Huang Gongwang, styled Zijiu, nicknamed "The Great Fool" and "One Peak," was a native of Jiangsu Province. He was born in 1269, during the Southern Song, and died in 1355, in the late Yuan. His forte was landscape painting, in which he was considered the best along with Wang Meng, Wu Zhen and Ni Zan. They had a profound influence on Ming and Qing styles. The painting reproduced here is quite typical of Huang Gongwang's style. Ni Zan, in his annotation on the painting, wrote, "This is a scroll to be proud of." The four Chinese characters for "Hill and Water in the Rain" were written by Lin Peng, a Yuan calligrapher.

45

46-2

46. *Watering and Feeding* by Ren Renfa Yuan painting, 29.7 x 186.5 cm. Ren Renfa (1255-1327) was a native of Qinglong (now Shanghai) of Songjiang Prefecture. He excelled in doing horses, in which he was considered the equal of the more famous Zhao Mengfu (see 44). Human figures and birds-and-flowers were also his forte. His other extant paintings include *Two Steeds, Zhang Guo Received by the Emperor* and *Scholar with a Horizontal Stringed Instrument*. Besides painting, he was also well versed in water conservation, to which he made important contributions during the mid-Yuan. He took part in the construction of the Tonghui and Huihe canals, directed the building of water conservancy projects in eastern Zhejiang Province and on the old course of the Wusong River, and on occasions supervised the blocking of breaches on the Yellow River banks. He is the author of the book *Questions and Answers on Water Conservancy in Western Zhejiang Province*.

46-3

46-1

Uprising of the Red Turbans

The ruling class of the Yuan Dynasty was made up of the Mongol nobility, which was the main body, the great landlords of the Han Chinese and the upper strata of other nationalities. This ruling class established a hierarchic system with the Mongols at the top, followed by their Central Asian allies (mostly Uygurs and other Turks) called the Semu, the Han Chinese of the Yellow River valley, and the so-called southerners (mostly Hans) who inhabited the Yangtze valley and areas further south. This system of inequality aggravated both national and class contradictions. Resistance and revolts broke out one after another and eventually led to a nationwide peasant uprising. In 1351, an uprising led by Liu Futong and Han Shantong, two former leaders of the White Lotus secret society, took place in Yingzhou (now Fuyang, Anhui Province). As the rebels wore red turbans, they were called the Red Turban army. They received widespread support. Guo Zixing, a former landlord, led an uprising in Haozhou (now Fengyang city, Anhui Province); Xu Shouhui, a cloth merchant, seized Qishui (now Xishui County, Hubei Province) from the Mongols; Zhang Shicheng, a salt trader, occupied Gaoyou (in present Jiangsu Province); and Feng Guozhen, a former official, rebelled in modern eastern Zhejiang Province. The Red Turban armies in the north and south quickly expanded in strength and began setting up their own local regimes. A peasant army led by Zhu Yuanzhang, a former poor peasant, with its base at Jiqing (now Nanjing, Jiangsu Province), gradually extended its control over most places in the south and, in 1368, Zhu proclaimed the establishment of a new dynasty called Ming. In the same year, his armies marched north, occupied Dadu and overthrew the Yuan.

47-1

47-2

48

47. Seal of 10,000-household commander's office Yuan relic, 7.8 cm square; unearthed at Zaozhuang, Shandong Province, in 1967. In 1351, an uprising led by Han Shantong and Liu Futong broke out in Yingzhou (now Fuyang, Anhui Province). It was temporarily checked by Yuan armies and Han Shantong was killed. Shortly afterward, when Yuan troops moved south to suppress the Red Turbans there, Liu Futong seized the opportunity to stage a comeback. He proclaimed Han Lin'er, Han Shantong's son, the emperor of a new regime called the Great Song, with its base at Bozhou (now Bo County, Anhui Province), changed the reign title to Longfeng (Dragon-Phoenix), and dispatched three columns north to continue the fight against the Yuan. His eastern and western columns entered the present provinces of Shandong and Shanxi while the middle column reached Tongzhou (now Tongxian, a part of Beijing), threatening Dadu, the Yuan capital. The administrative setup of this Great Song regime was very similar to that of the Yuan in both name and structure. It had a council called Zhongshu Sheng at the central level, under which were six ministries in charge of civil offices, census and revenue, rites, military affairs, criminal justice and public works. (Other ministries may have been contemplated but were not set up.) Its military ranks included marshals, general administrators and commanders of 10,000-household, 1,000-household and 100-household units. The bronze seal shown in the photo bears a legend carved in relief. It consists

49

of six characters in seal script that read in translation: "Office seal of commander of 10,000-household unit." On the back of the seal is the same legend but carved in intaglio in regular script. Two other legends on the back, also in intaglio, read: "Made by the Ministry of Rites of the Zhongshu Sheng" and "... day, 2nd month, 5th year of the Longfeng reign." At one side of the seal is another legend, with five characters, that may be translated as "Ref. Duanzi 17." This was a military seal cast by the Ministry of Rites of the Great Song regime.

48. *Longfeng tongbao* coin Yuan currency, 2.4 cm in diameter. This bronze coin was minted after the establishment of Han Lin'er's regime and bears his reign title.

49. *Tianqi tongbao* coin Yuan currency, 3.4 cm in diameter. In 1351 Xu Shouhui led an uprising in eastern Hubei Province. He quickly occupied Qishui (now Xishui County, Hubei Province) and established a regime called Tianwan with the reign title Zhiping. His power at one time extended over the modern provinces of Hubei, Hunan, Jiangxi, Anhui, Fujian, Jiangsu and Zhejiang, but he overstretched his strength and only two

52

years later was defeated by the Yuan. In 1356, when the main force of the Yuan armies moved north to fight Han Lin'er, he made a comeback and, with Hanyang (now part of Wuhan, Hubei Province) as his new capital, extended his power into the provinces of Jiangxi and Hunan. In 1358 he changed his reign title to Tianqi and minted *Tianqi tongbao* coins. In the following year, however, Chen Youliang, one of his officers, forced him to move his capital to Jiangzhou (now Jiujiang, Jiangxi Province) and change his reign

50-1

50-2

title to Tianding. Thus the reign title Tianqi was used for only a short time. Not very many coins were minted during this time and an even smaller number have survived, the one shown here being a rare and precious find.

50. Seal of army marshal Yuan relic, 7.7 cm square, 9.6 cm high. The legend on this bronze seal consists of six characters in seal script carved in relief. It reads: "Seal of army marshal." On the back of the seal is the same legend carved in intaglio in regular script and two other legends that read: "Made by the Ministry of Rites, Zhongshu Sheng" and "... day, ...

month, 2nd year of Dayi reign." Dayi was the reign title of a regime set up by Chen Youliang, a Red Turban leader in the south who had served under Xu Shouhui (see 49). In 1360 he murdered Xu Shouhui and proclaimed himself emperor, changed the name of his regime to Da Han (Great Han) and the reign title to Dayi. At the height of his power, he controlled large parts of Jiangxi, Hubei and Hunan provinces and was one of the most powerful leaders of the peasant movements. This seal, cast in 1361, was his army seal.

51. *Dayi tongbao* coin Yuan currency, 2.7 cm in diameter; minted by Chen Youliang's regime and bearing his reign title.

52. *Tianyou tongbao* coin Yuan currency, 2.5 cm in diameter. In 1353 Zhang Shicheng led a peasant uprising in Taizhou (in present Jiangsu

51

Province). In the following year he occupied Gaoyou (also in Jiangsu Province) and set up a regime which he called Da Zhou (Great Zhou), with Tianyou as his reign title. Shortly afterward he moved his capital to Suzhou (present Suzhou city in Jiangxi Province) where he continued to expand his military strength. At one time his domain extended to Jining (in modern Shandong Province) in the north, to northern Anhui Province in the west, and to Shaoxing (in Zhejiang Province) in the south. He was, however, a vacillating person. In the beginning he opposed the Yuan; subsequently he accepted the amnesty of the Yuan court; later he rebelled again. On many occasions he also attacked other insurgent armies. In 1367 he was defeated and captured by Zhu Yuanzhang, the man who later founded the Ming Dynasty, and committed suicide while in captivity. *Tianyou tongbao* was a coin with his reign title, minted after he set up his regime.

Ming Dynasty

(1368—1644)

The Ming Dynasty was first set up by Zhu Yuanzhang in Nanjing. In 1421, the 19th year of the Yongle reign of the third Ming emperor, it moved its capital to Beijing. 16 Ming emperors ruled the country successively for a total of 277 years. Zhu Yuanzhang, the founder, after proclaiming himself emperor, had to fight wars of conquest for another 20 years before unifying the country. The frontiers of the Ming empire at the height of its power extended to the Wudi River in the north, the Sea of Japan in the northeast, and Hami in the west. The vast southwest, including Tibet, and the numerous islands in the East China and South China seas were also part of the empire. The Ming government adopted measures to encourage farming

and textile-weaving. It promoted the practice of using garrison troops to till the land where they were stationed, resettled large numbers of peasants on virgin territory, built water conservation projects, and reduced the burdens of taxation and corvée labor on the peasants. In the handicrafts, artisans all over the country used to be sent to the capital by turns to work for the government. The work was hard and gave rise to widespread dissatisfaction, including many desertions.

The Ming government, therefore, adopted a policy under which artisans who did not want to work for the government could pay a sum of money instead. This freed them from the fetters of officialdom, and handicraft production was able to recover very quickly. In the process, the buds of a capitalist mode of production began to appear. Zhu Yuanzhang strengthened the authority of the central government, putting both political and military power in the hands of the emperor. Thus autocratic centralized rule was further enhanced. At the beginning of the 15th century, Zheng He, a eunuch, made seven voyages to the "Western Oceans" (a historic term for places in southern Asia and Africa), promoting friendly relations between the Ming court and various Asian-African countries. Towards the end of the Ming Dynasty, eunuchs were in complete control of the government, which had become exceedingly corrupt. This coupled with frequent natural disasters caused widespread discontent. In the northeast, the Manchu nationality became powerful. In the west, peasant uprisings led by Li Zicheng and Zhang Xianzhong spread like prairie fires, ultimately toppling the rule of the Ming.

Establishment of the Ming Dynasty

In 1368, Zhu Yuanzhang established the Ming Dynasty at Yingtian (now Nanjing, Jiangsu Province). He had unified the vast area that encompassed the modern provinces of Fujian and Guangdong and the present Guangxi Autonomous Region. In August the same year he captured the Yuan capital, Dadu, overthrowing the Yuan Dynasty, and subsequently occupied the provinces of Shanxi, Henan, Shaanxi and Gansu. In 1371, the separatist regime of Da Xia (Great Xia) in Sichuan Province surrendered; in 1381, the remnants of Yuan power in Yunnan were crushed; and by 1387, when Nahachu, chief of Mongol forces entrenched in northeastern Liaoning Province, surrendered, the whole country was unified. Meanwhile, Zhu Yuanzhang had taken measures to reform the political, economic and military institutions of the Yuan and its culture and customs, with emphasis on the abolition of the Yuan policy of ethnic discrimination and oppression. At the central level, both the Zhongshu Sheng, which functioned like a cabinet, and the prime minister system were abolished and all power was concentrated in the hands of the emperor. In the economic sphere, the Ming government pursued a policy of giving the people time to rest and recuperate and reformed the systems of taxation and corvée labor so that both agriculture and the handicrafts were able to recover and develop.

Strengthening of Autocratic Centralized Power

After establishing the Ming Dynasty, Zhu Yuanzhang abolished the Zhongshu Sheng (cabinet) and prime minister system, but gave wider powers to the six ministries in charge of civil offices, census and revenue, rites, military affairs, criminal justice and public works, which were responsible directly to the emperor. In the provinces, he set up three organs in charge of civil, judicial and military affairs respectively. He established a *wei-suo* system in the army. A *wei* consisted of roughly 5,600 men; a 1,000-household *suo*, 1,120 men; and a 100-household *suo*, 112 men. At the central level he created a Five-Army Command in charge of military training and administration. All power to direct, deploy and move troops was in the hands of the emperor.

To strengthen the legal system, he ordered the compilation of the *Da Ming Lu* (*Codes of the Great Ming*) and *Da Gao* (*Great Imperial Mandate*). To tighten control over household registration, taxation and corvée labor, he had two registers compiled for each administrative region. One was called the *Yellow Register* and tabulated each household in the region, giving the names of its members, its landed property, and its share in taxes and corvée labor. The other, called the *Fish-Scale Register*, contained detailed drawings of the land owned by each household.

53. Portrait of Zhu Yuanzhang Zhu Yuanzhang (1328-1398) was a native of Zhongli, Haozhou (now Fengyang, Anhui Province). He came from a poor family and in his youth lived for a time as a monk. In 1352 he joined the uprising against the Yuan led by Guo Zixing, serving as the leader of a ten-man squad. Through his courage and

53

resourcefulness, he won the confidence of Guo Zixing and eventually became a leader of the uprising. He captured Jiqing

54

(now Nanjing), making it his base. Then, adopting the strategy proposed by his counselor Zhu Shen to "build high walls, store large supplies of grain, and defer proclaiming himself emperor," he gradually extended his sphere of power through fighting other separatist regimes. In 1368 he proclaimed himself emperor at Nanjing and adopted the dynastic title Great Ming and reign title Hongwu. He sent troops north to overthrow the Yuan, then fought wars of conquest in the northwest, southeast and southwest, eventually unifying the country. He abolished the Zhongshu Sheng (cabinet) and prime minister system, concentrating all political and military power in his own hands. He adopted measures to revive and develop agriculture, which enabled the nation's economy to recover. To maintain his autocratic rule, however, he created a large number of unjust cases and executed

many of his subordinates who had served him well. In 1398 he died in Nanjing and was buried at Xiaoling, Zhongshan.

54. Bronze badge of *xiao-wei* officer of the Imperial City, Nanjing Ming relic, 10.5 cm wide, 12.9 cm high; unearthed at the site of a Ming palace in Nanjing, Jiangsu Province. The Imperial City in Nanjing was built by Zhu Yuanzhang. It consisted mainly of government organs and imperial gardens. In 1369 an office of the commander of the imperial guards was set up there. Under its command were five contingents called the Center, Left, Right, Front and Rear Guard. In 1373 gold badges, actually gold-plated bronze badges, were made for the guards to wear. These badges were in the custody of a special department. The guards wore them when on duty and had to return them when off duty. In 1382. a special force called the Embroidered Uniform Guard was set up. It was the emperor's personal bodyguard and had the power to inspect, investigate and make arrests. It comprised 14 departments commanded by generals, *lishi* (literally "strong men") and *xiao-wei*. The *xiao-wei* were the lowest ranking officers, whose duty was to ensure the safety of the Imperial City. They had to check the passes of all who entered or left the city and would be severely punished for any negligence. The badge shown here was worn by a *xiao-wei* on night duty.

55. Seal of 100-household unit of the Rear 1,000-Household Guard of the Xi'an Right Guards Ming relic, 7 cm square, 8.4 cm high, cast by the Ming government. The 100-household unit, or *suo*, was the basic unit of the Ming army. It consisted of 112 men. Ten 100-household *suo* formed one 1,000-household *suo*, and five 1,000-household *suo* (called front, rear,

left, right and center) formed a wei (guard) of 5,600 men. Each 100-household suo was headed by two men called *zongqi*, or chief banners, and ten *xiaoqi*, or small banners. Zhu Yuanzhang, after unifying the country, made his sons princes and stationed them in different parts of the country. To ensure their safety, he had a command post for guards set up in each fief. Under each command post were three contingents of guards, called the left, right and center guards. The Xi'an Right Guards was the bodyguard of Zhu Shuang, Prince of Qin, who was Zhu Yuanzhang's second son. This square bronze seal was cast in 1378, the year Zhu Shuang became the feudatory of Xi'an.

55

56. Bronze badge for night patrolman in the command post of the Beiping Provisional Capital Ming relic, 12 cm wide, 14 cm high. In 1387 the Ming government established a command post for the Beiping Provisional Capital at Daning (near Ningcheng County in the modern Inner Mongolia Autonomous Region). As Daning was in the far north and confronted remnants of the Mongol forces of the deposed Yuan Dynasty, it was necessary to set up a strong command post there. This post was garrisoned by 16 *wei*, well over 100,000 men, under the command of the Prince of Ning. When Chengzu, the third Ming emperor, succeeded to the throne, he transferred the Prince of Ning to Nanchang in Jiangxi Province and changed the Beiping Provisional Capital Command into the Daning Capital Command with its headquarters at Baoding (in modern Hebei Province). This bronze badge was worn by guards of the Daning command when on night duty. Cast on the badge is the legend "Bronze badge for night patrolman of the Beiping Provisional Capital Command, Ref. Suzi 464." On the back is a single character meaning "order."

56-1

56-2

57

57. Portrait of Zhu Di Zhu Di (1360-1424) was Zhu Yuanzhang's fourth son. He was the Prince of Yan and commanded a strong garrison at Beiping. When Zhu Yuanzhang died, his eldest grandson, Zhu Yunwen, succeeded to the throne as Emperor Huidi. To remove the threats posed by his many uncles, he enlisted the help of his chief ministers and with their support abolished one by one the various feudatories his grandfather had set up. Zhu Di, however, rebelled and after four years of warfare captured Nanjing and made himself emperor. After succeeding to the throne, he personally led five expeditions to the north and subsequently moved his capital to Beijing in order to prevent attempts at restoration by remnants of the Yuan Dynasty. Meanwhile, to expand economic and cultural exchange with neighboring countries and other countries in Asia and Africa, he dispatched Zheng He, a eunuch, with a large fleet to visit places in southeast, south and southwest Asia and east Africa. To resolve the problem of shipping grain to Beijing, he mobilized the people to dredge the Huitong Canal so that the waters of the north-south Grand Canal could flow unobstructed from Hangzhou to Beijing, bringing over two million hectoliters of southern grain to the capital each year and facilitating economic and cultural exchange between north and south. On the literary front, he organized over 3,000 scholars to compile the largest encyclopedia in Chinese history, the *Yongle Encyclopedia.* In 1424, he undertook his fifth northern expedition but died of illness on the way. He was 65, had reigned for 22 years and was buried at Changling, Beijing, with the posthumous title Chengzu.

58. Ivory badge worn by a "constant follower" of the emperor Ming relic, 5.2 cm wide, 14 cm high. In the eleven imperial offices of the inner court of the Ming palace were officials of the sixth rank who served as "constant followers" of the emperor. The badge shown here was a permit worn by these officials, allowing them to freely enter and leave the inner court. It was made of ivory and the user hung it on his waist belt. Inscribed on one side of the badge were four characters that mean "constant follower of emperor," and on the other side were two characters that mean "serious." The gates of the palaces in the Imperial City were heavily guarded and there was a strict system of checking people entering or leaving them. A pass for entering or leaving a palace was made of ivory or bronze, with directions and sometimes the name of the user inscribed on it.

59. Palace City in Beijing Silk painting done in the early years of the Ming Dynasty. Construction of this Palace City, also called the Forbidden City, in Beijing began in 1406 and was basically completed in 1420. It stood a short distance to the south of the palaces in the Yuan capital Dadu. Its scale, shape and names were all based on those of the Ming palaces in Nanjing. Although rebuilt and enlarged during later periods, its basic form and structure were not changed. It consisted of two parts. The front part comprised the Hall of Reverence for Heaven, Canopy Hall and Hall of Circumspection, which formed the main body, and the Hall of Literary Excellence to the east and Hall of Military Prowess to the west. It was where the emperor held court and presided over important ceremonies. The back part was where the royal family lived and performed their daily tasks; the principal buildings here were the Palace of Heavenly Purity, Hall of Peace and Palace of Earthly Tranquillity. According to studies made, the figure standing below the Gate of Indebtedness to Heaven (now called the Gate of Heavenly Peace) in the painting is Kuai Xiang, the designer of the gate. He was a native of Wuxian, Suzhou (in modern Jiangsu Province) and was originally a carpenter. During the Yongle years (1403-1424) he took part in the building of the Beijing Palace City and later was made an official in the Ministry of Works.

60. Jingtai bronze cannon   Ming smoothbore firearm, called a *chong*, length 26.1 cm, muzzle diameter 10 cm, base diameter 9.1 cm. It consists of two parts, a powder magazine and a tube. On the powder magazine is a small hole for the insertion of a fuse. Ming armies first used such weapons during the Yongle years (1403-1424). They varied in size. Larger ones were fired from carriages and were used to defend cities and forts. Smaller ones were mounted on supports and used as offensive weapons during attacks or charges in battle. The Ming government established two bureaus, the War Bureau and Munitions Bureau, specially to study and make such *chong* cannons. Those made during the early Ming could fire three shots in succession and had a range of 300 *bu* (about 450 meters). The ones made in the late Ming were much larger. They were about two meters long, weighed approximately 700 kg (even lighter ones weighed about 80 kg), could fire ten shots in succession and had a firing range of 700 *bu* (over 1,000 meters). The *chong* cannon shown here was made in 1450, the first year of the Jingtai reign, a period of national crisis and war. In the previous year, the Wala tribes of western

60-2

Mongolia had defeated a Ming army at Tumubao and captured the Ming emperor Zhu Qizhen. Taking their captive with them, they attacked Beijing but were stopped by the stubborn resistance of the capital's soldiers and civilians led by Yu Qian (later acclaimed as a national hero), and eventually were defeated and forced to retreat.

60-1

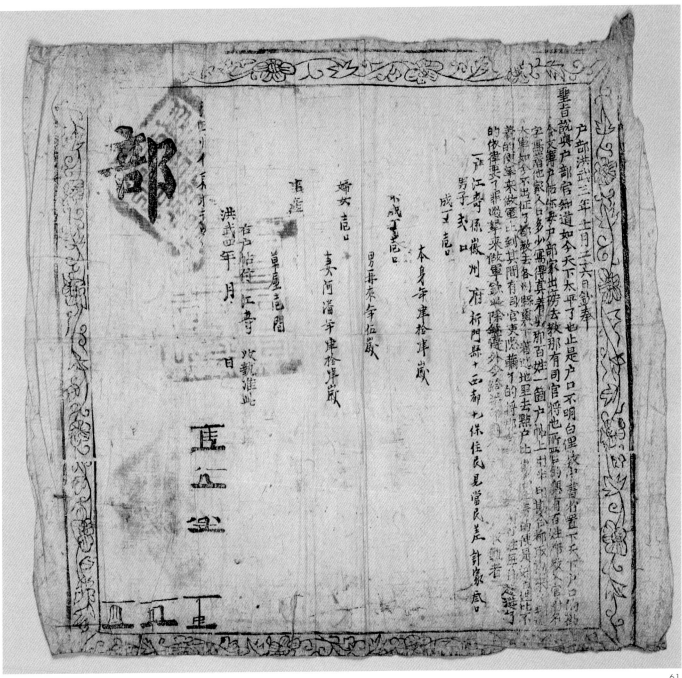

61

61. Household certificate of Jiang Shou of Qimen County, Huizhou Prefecture

Ming document, 33.9 x 35.8 cm. Beginning in 1370, the third year of the Hongwu reign, the Ming government instituted a household registration system for the country. The household registers were kept by the government, but a registration card, called a household certificate, was issued to each household. The one shown here was issued to Jiang Shou of Qimen County, Huizhou Prefecture (now Xi County, Anhui Province). To make sure that taxes were paid and corvée exacted, the Ming government in its early years undertook a nationwide survey of land and entered the results into a book called the *Fish-Scale Register,* which was used for the levying of grain taxes. Later, in 1381, it published the official *Yellow Register* as the basis for taxation and corvée. To compile this official register, it issued forms that each and every household was required to fill in, giving the name, native place, sex, age, address, profession and property of each of its members. On the basis of these forms, the government compiled a separate register for each county in the country. It was made out in four copies, which were kept by the county, prefectural, provincial and central governments respectively, and was called the *Yellow Register* because the cover of the copy for the central government was yellow. A new *Yellow Register* was issued every ten years. On the basis of this register, the Ming government established a *li-jia* system at the grassroots level, organizing every 110 households into a *li* and every 10 households into a *jia.*

Administration of Border Regions

The Ming Dynasty established defense zones known as *wei-suo* in the border regions. It appointed as governors of those zones ethnic minority leaders who were responsible directly to the central government. This policy helped to consolidate and develop the multinationality country. During the Yongle years (1403-1424), remnant forces of the Mongol Yuan Dynasty were a constant threat to the rule of the Ming. Zhu Di, the third Ming emperor, undertook five expeditions to subdue them, inflicting serious setbacks to the three large Mongol tribes of Wuliangha, Tartar and Wala. In 1409, he set up a military post at Nurkan in the northeast, which commanded 184 *wei* (a *wei* was an army unit of about 5,600 men). In its early years the Ming Dynasty also strengthened its control over Tibet. It summoned Tibetan religious leaders to the capital to take part in religious activities, appointed them to official posts, and gave them power to administer the local affairs of Tibet. Additionally, it set up markets for trade in tea and horses at places where Han and Tibetan territory joined. It also set up various governmental organs in places inhabited by minorities in the south and southwest, all of which were administered by native upper class leaders. Beginning in the Yongle years, it abolished in some minority areas the *tusi* system, under which local leaders used to serve on a hereditary basis, and replaced it with a new system that required all leaders to be appointed by the Ming government.

62. Painting (section) showing the successful quelling of a rebellion in the northwest Ming relic, original scroll 43.8 x 972.2 cm painted on colored silk. It was preserved by descendants of Li Wenzhong, a nephew of Zhu Yuanzhang, and regarded as a "prized heirloom of the family of the Prince of Qiyang." It is a historic painting that shows how Ming troops put down a rebellion by ethnic minorities in the northwest during the Wanli years (1573-1619). It depicts events that took place in 1575, the third year of the Wanli reign, when a Western Fan tribe in southwestern Gansu Province attacked Taozhou (now Lintan County, Gansu Province) and the Ming government dispatched the military governor of Guyuan (in the modern Ningxia Hui Autonomous Region) with troops from Hezhou (now Linxia County, Gansu Province) to put down the rebellion. The complete scroll consists of 14 scenes. The first scene is titled "Dispatching Troops at the Guyuan Camp"; the second, "Liu Boxie, Commander of Guyuan's Reserves"; the third, "Sun Guochen, Military Governor of Shaanxi"; and the fourth, "Baihua Ridge." The 14th or last scene shows the governor-general of Guyuan rewarding his troops. The customs and architectural styles of northwestern ethnic minorities during the Ming as reflected in the painting fully accord with documentary records. Thus the scroll is a valuable piece of reference for the study of military affairs and folk customs of the Ming. The photo shows only the first and fourth scenes.

62-1

白化嶺

62-2

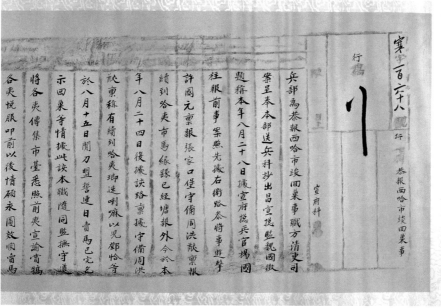

63

63. Manuscript (section) on the reopening of the Mongol-Han horse market at Zhangjiakou Ming manuscript issued by the Ministry of War in 1637, the 10th year of the Chongzhen reign, at the request of local officials and with the approval of Ming emperor Sizong. In order to carry out regular barter trade, the Ming Dynasty since its founding had set up markets at key points where Han territory bordered on that of ethnic minorities. Such markets were called "horse markets" and were administered by the government. Merchants of the interior offered their tea, salt, cloth and iron tools in exchange for horses, cattle and sheep which were the special products of minority regions. This kind of trade was commonly called "tea-horse trade." Thirteen horse markets were set up in the north, two of which were at Datong and Zhangjiakou where trade was carried out regularly with various Mongol tribes. During the mid-16th century, friction rose between the khan of the Mongol Tartar tribe and the Ming government and the latter closed the markets at those two places. They were reopened during the Longqing years (1567-1572) when a peace agreement was reached between the two sides. The manuscript reproduced here was a product of the peace process. It set forth the advantages of reopening the Zhangjiakou market, observing that "Now that the market has reopened, official and merchants have flocked to the place, and goods and silver are as plentiful as stars in the sky. Not only can officers and soldiers again mount fast steeds; the local people,

too, have benefited from the trade. Thus in less than a year the barrier has taken on a new look and wornout troops are energized."

64. Xuande bronze bell and pestle Ming Buddhist objects. Overall height of bell 19.5 cm, mouth diameter 9.5 cm; overall length of pestle 12.7 cm. These two

Buddhist objects were presented to a temple in Lhasa, Tibet, by the Ming government during the Xuande years (1426-1435). On the 60th birthday of Qing emperor Qianlong, the Dalai Lama returned them to the Qing court as birthday gifts for the emperor and they were preserved in the Qing royal palace.

64-1

Economy and Social Life

The Ming government adopted a number of measures to assist the recovery and development of the nation's economy during its early years. It resettled large numbers of people in order to open up new land, encouraged the reclamation of wasteland, promoted the practice of using troops to cultivate the land on which they were stationed, reduced the burdens of taxation and corvée on the peasants, and thus was able to raise agricultural production. In areas south of the Yangtze, the acreage devoted to planting rice was enlarged and two-harvest and three-harvest paddy were widely cultivated, increasing the yield per unit area. Cotton growing was extended to all parts of the country. Increasing the acreage for industrial crops provided more raw materials for the development of handicrafts. A system under which craftsmen served in the capital by turns gave them time for their own productive activities. By the mid-Ming, this system was modified to allow craftsmen to pay a certain amount of money in lieu of service in the capital, which gave them even more time to pursue their own interests. Spinning and weaving, ceramics, metallurgy and shipbuilding all made great progress during the Ming, contributing to the rapid development of the nation's economy. By the mid- and late Ming, buds of capitalism had appeared in some places.

Agriculture

Early in the Ming Dynasty, the government adopted a policy of letting the people recuperate. As a result, more than 1.8 million hectares of wasteland were reclaimed and the total cultivated area reached 8.56 million hectares. To increase the crop yield, the government organized the people to build irrigation works, resulting in an enlarged irrigated area. The grain delivered as tax to the state reached 20.88 million dan (1 dan = 1 hectoliter) in 1385, the 18th year of the Hongwu reign, and 32.78 million dan in 1393, the 26th year. A scene of prosperity prevailed, with granaries everywhere full to the brim.

65. License to reclaim wasteland in Zhili
Official paper, 60.2 x 46 cm, Ming Dynasty. This license was issued to Huang Xuansheng, a peasant of Qimen County, Huizhou Prefecture, Zhili Province (now Qimen County, Anhui Province). On the paper were noted the name of the plot of land to be reclaimed, its area, geographical position and the boundaries on its four sides, as well as the amount of grain to be paid in tax after three years of tax exemption. It also stated that the peasant Huang Xuansheng was entitled to keep the land as his permanent property. All this conforms to the policy on land reclamation adopted by the early Ming government.

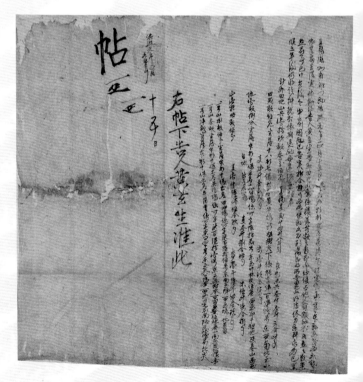

66

peasant households from Dayangdu in Zezhou (now Jincheng, Shanxi Province) to Shuanglanchi, Jixian, Weihui Prefecture (now Jixian, Henan Province). In the Ming Dynasty, 110 peasant households constituted one *li,* a unit of civil administration. Engraved on the tablet are the names of all the peasants and the chief of the *li.* The tablet is now kept in Shuanglanchi, Jixian, Henan Province.

66. *Jinhua* silver ingot   Relic of the Ming Dynasty. In the first years of the Ming Dynasty, the government collected grain taxes from the peasants twice a year, in summer and in autumn. The taxes were paid in kind, mostly wheat in summer and rice in autumn. Later, with economic development, this was changed. Beginning in 1436, the first year of the Zhengtong reign, peasants in the area south of the Yangtze River were ordered to pay grain taxes in silver coins instead of rice or wheat, and the money thus paid became known as *jinhua* silver. Each year the local government had the *jinhua* silver coins cast into ingots before turning them over to the Board of Revenue. The ingot in the picture, weighing 50 taels, was delivered to the Board of Revenue by the Fujian government in 1588, the 16th year of the Wanli reign. Engraved on the concave side of the ingot were the name of the local government, the category of tax, weight, loss in casting, as well as the names of the official concerned and the silversmith.

67. Rubbing of a tablet commemorating a mass migration to Jixian   Relic of the Ming Dynsaty, 110 cm long, 55.8 cm wide. When the Ming Dynasty was established after a decade-long cruel war with the Mongols, agricultural production in the north and the Central Plains seriously declined, with large tracts of land lying waste and many places sparsely populated. Zhu Yuanzhang, the founding emperor of the Ming Dynasty, ordered reclamation of land on a nationwide scale. Peasants were given the land they restored to production, with no tax due for the first three years. Frontier soldiers were ordered to open up new fields, with seeds and cattle provided by the government. Unemployed peasants were moved to sparsely populated areas to reclaim land, with seeds, cattle and traveling expenses provided by the government. The tablet in the picture, erected in Shuanglanchi in 1391, the 24th year of the Hongwu reign, records the migration of all 110

68-1

68-2

68. "Tilling at Dawn" Colored painting on silk, 172 x 101.9 cm, Ming Dynasty. This painting depicts the busy spring plowing season in an area south of the Yangtze River. Dawn breaks over rows of thatched huts at the foot of a hill. A few peasants are seen tilling a rice paddy, while other villagers, men and women, old and young, are busy with their farm work within or without the thatched huts.

69."The Yellow River and the Grand Canal"
(section of a colored drawing on silk)   Entire
drawing, 45 x 1959 cm, Ming Dynasty. The
Yellow River, the second longest in China,
runs from west to east in north China,
whereas the Grand Canal, starting from
Hangzhou in the southeast and terminating
in Beijing in the north, is a man-made
waterway cutting through and thus linking
the Yangtze and Yellow rivers. To facilitate
shipping grain north, two channels in the
system of the Grand Canal were dug during
the Zhiyuan reign of the Yuan Dynasty—
Huitong in Shandong Province and Tonghui
in Beijing—but both were silted up shortly
thereafter. It was not until the Ming Dynasty
that 300,000 laborers from Shandong,
Xuzhou, Yingtian and Zhenjiang were
mobilized to dredge the Huitong Channel,
and the Grand Canal was made navigable.
The canal, which carried three to four million
hectoliters of grain each year, became a
lifeline for the Ming Dynasty. People in the
Ming-Qing period often associated the Yellow
River with the Grand Canal, evidenced by the
illustration shown here. The east-of-Kaifeng
section of the Yellow River suffered from
frequent breaches of dykes, floods, and
changes in the river's course as a result of
the large amount of silt carried by the river,
and whenever such events occurred, traffic
on the Grand Canal was suspended.

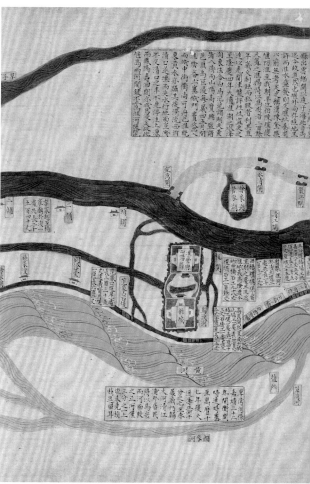

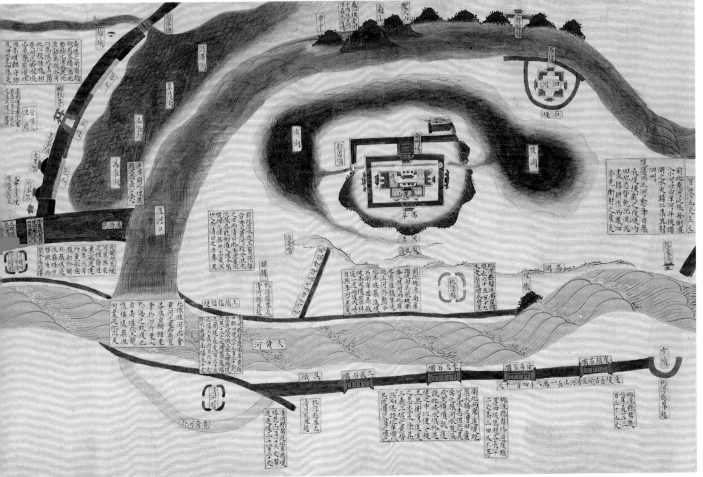

Handicraft Industry

Early in the Ming Dynasty, it was decreed that a certain proportion of land should be planted with hemp and mulberry trees and that hemp fabric and silk floss should be included in the taxes paid by the peasants to the government. This led to a sericulture boom all over the country. A number of cities became centers of China's silk industry, such as Huzhou, Nanjing and Hangzhou in the lower Yangtze valley, Lu'an in Shanxi Province, and Chengdu and Langzhong in Sichuan Province. Improvements in looms brought about increased silk production and a wide variety of designs and colors of silk fabric. Cotton was widely planted in the country; weaving cotton cloth became a major cottage industry among the peasants. Songjiang Prefecture in the lower Yangtze Valley became the center for China's cotton fabric.

In porcelain making, the Ming Dynasty succeeded in producing articles in a variety of shapes and colors. The town of Jingdezhen boasted 58 state kilns and over 900 private ones turning out large quantities of exquisite porcelain. The Dehua Kiln in Fujian Province was famous for its white porcelain and porcelain sculpture.

The iron-smelting sector flourished also, with Zunhua in Hebei, Yangcheng in Shanxi and Foshan in Guangdong as its three centers. During the Hongwu reign the production quota for iron set by the government reached nine million kilograms a year. The dynasty also produced a large quantity of copper, sufficient to meet the great demand for coins, bells and Buddhist statues.

70. *Zhuanghua* gauze decorated with magic fungi, coiled dragons, and the Chinese character for longevity   Relic of the Ming Dynasty; unearthed from the Dingling tomb in Changping, Beijing. *Zhuanghua,* a type of silk fabric much in vogue during the Ming Dynasty, was woven with weft in a multi-colored design. The weaving of this fabric was very complex. *Sha* (gauze), *luo* (leno), *juan* (thin, tough silk) and *chou* (silk in general) could all be woven in this way. With its ingenious design and magnificent colors, it was considered the best of all silk fabrics. A great variety of silk gauze was produced in the Ming Dynasty, varying according to the place of origin. The coiled-dragon design was a feature of traditional Chinese silk fabric.

71. Brocade with colored cloud-dragon-seawater design on a black background   Relic of the Ming Dynasty, 38 x 13 cm. It was ruled early in the Ming Dynasty that mulberry trees should be planted and silkworms bred in all places suited for sericulture, otherwise a double tax on silk floss would be imposed. This spurred rapid development in silk production. In a short period the provinces of Zhejiang, Jiangsu and Sichuan became the silk bases, and the cities of Hangzhou, Huzhou, Nanjing, Suzhou, Luzhou (now Changzhi, Shanxi Province) and Baoning (now Langzhong, Sichuan Province), bases for silk weaving. A Textile Bureau on the local level was set up during the Ming Dynasty. Silks for government use were produced by state workshops, whereas those sold all over the country came from private workshops. Because of improvements in looms, the Ming silks surpassed previous periods in quality. The brocade in the picture shows the high quality of Ming products.

72

73

74

72. *Ling* (silk damask) with golden floral design on a water-blue background   Relic of the Ming Dynasty, 39 x 14 cm. *Ling,* a traditional type of silk fabric, was an alternating twill weave, featuring a checkerboard design or reversible twill pattern. Other types were *si, chou, luo, duan* and *juan.* The Ming Dynasty developed many new varieties, with a production base for each. Further improvements were made in the techniques of printing and dyeing silk and cotton fabrics. Several dozen species of plants were used in dyeing at the time. The government had a department in charge of pigments and an office to handle the fabric printing and dyeing just for clothing of the imperial family.

73. Cotton print with floral design on a blue background   Relic of the Ming Dynasty, 35.1 x 14.3 cm. During the Ming Dynasty, the cotton textile industry developed rapidly all over the country, especially in the lower Yangtze valley, where Songjiang became the country's cotton textile center. Cotton prints were always in fashion. One could find cotton cloth printing and dyeing workshops in most cities and towns. Two methods were used in printing and dyeing. The cotton print pictured, on which the pattern is as brilliant as if freshly painted, was made by stretching the cloth over an engraved block and applying colors to it.

74. Songjiang cloth   Relic of the Ming Dynasty, 229 x 57.5 cm; unearthed in Fengxian, Jiangsu Province. In the late Yuan Dynasty a woman named Huang Daopo introduced the cotton textile technology of Hainan into Songjiang (now Shanghai). After that, Songjiang rose quickly to eminence and became a national center for trading in cotton textiles, with merchants coming all over the country. Songjiang cloth, a highly finished product, was spotlessly white. The famous brands of Songjiang cloth were Meizhi, Sanling, Feihua and Youdun, all far surpassing the cloth produced elsewhere.

75. Blue and white vase with cloud-dragon-seawater design Ornament, 45.8 cm high, rim 8.1 cm in diameter, base 14.8 cm in diameter, Ming Dynasty. This vase, fired in an imperial kiln in Jingdezhen, has a round mouth, a long neck, an oblate belly and a flat bottom. The neck is covered with a design of lotus and curved grass, whereas the belly features two white dragons amid wild waves on the sea. It is a typical example of the blue and white porcelain of the Xuande period (1426-1435). This type of porcelain, which matured during the Yongle and Xuande reigns, is famous for its thin body, elegant shape, dignified decoration, and attractive blue and white colors.

76. Two-eared blue and white vase with interlocking branch design Ornament, 19.6 cm high, Ming Dynasty. The interlocking branch motif was very common on Ming porcelain. Ceramics covered with plant designs appear fresh and elegant.

77. Blue and white jar with pomegranate and magic fungus design fired in the Xuande period Ornament, 19 cm high, rim 6.3 cm in diameter, base 9.5 cm in diameter, Ming Dynasty. A new product of the Xuande period, this jar is covered with a design of pomegranates and magic mushrooms, symbolizing jubilation and longevity. With a fine body, unique shape, lively decoration, and rich, brilliant glaze, the jar influenced later generations of porcelain producers. During the Yongle and Xuande reigns, Zheng He, an envoy sent by the Ming government to Southeast Asia and the Indian Ocean, brought to China high-quality Persian glazes for making blue and white porcelain. After that, imported glazes dominated for the blue and white porcelain fired in state kilns. It was found that porcelain articles made with such glazes looked clearer and livelier and had a sharper contrast of colors.

78

78. Three-handled white jar with veiled decoration Container, 9.4 cm high, 10.3 cm in diameter at the top and 14.3 at the bottom, Ming Dynasty. This jar, made during the Yongle reign (1403-1424), is covered with a glaze of such a lovely white hue that it is called "sweet white." The "sweetness" was produced by reducing the iron content in the white glaze to the minimum and by applying a translucent glaze to the body in the course of firing at a high temperature. The white porcelain of the Ming Dynasty is highly valued.

79. Plain tricolor vase with chrysanthemum-shaped handles Ornament, 36.3 cm high, 10.5 cm in diameter at the top and 11.5 at the bottom, Ming Dynasty. Plain tricolor porcelain, developed during the Ming Dynasty, was made by applying painted or incised decorations in yellow, green and purple to a fired white body and then coating it with a layer of snow white glaze before refiring at a low temperature. This type of porcelain, sometimes with decorations on a yellow, green or purple background, appears clear, bright and elegant.

79

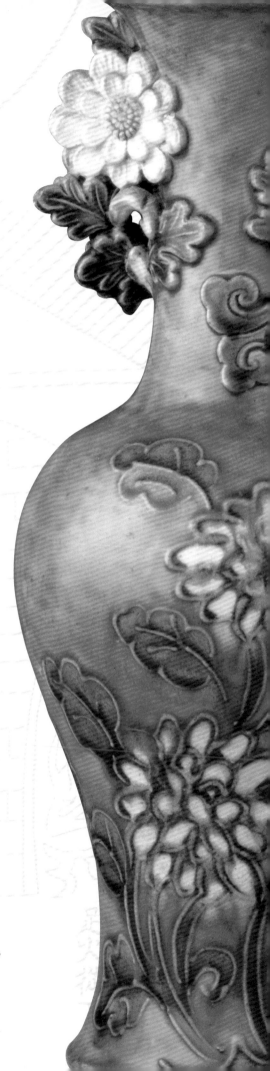

80

80. *Ji* blue plate of the Xuande period
Container, 4.6 cm high, 19.8 cm in diameter at the top and 12.2 at the bottom, Ming Dynasty. *Ji* blue was a blue glaze derived from cobalt. It was first used in the tricolor pottery of the Tang Dynasty. During the Yuan Dynasty it began to appear on single-glazed porcelain. By the Xuande period of the Ming Dynasty, porcelain with this glaze, known as "*ji* blue," became very popular. Together with "sweet white" and "*ji* red," "*ji* blue" is considered as one of the three best types of porcelain from the Xuande period. Produced in a single firing at a high temperature, *ji* blue porcelain features a thick, well-spread glaze with no cracks, and veiled or incised decoration, sometimes edged with pure gold.

81. *Doucai* jar with flower-and-butterfly design of the Chenghua period (with illustration showing the making of porcelain in the Ming Dynasty) Relic of the Ming Dynasty, 9.3 cm high, 7.4 cm in diameter at the top and 9.4 at the bottom. *Doucai* in Chinese means vying for glamor. *Doucai* porcelain is so called because it is decorated underglaze and overglaze with patterns in many colors, seeming to compete for beauty. Generally speaking, a *doucai* article was made by applying decoration in red, yellow, green and purple on a fired blue-and-white vessel and then refiring it at a low temperature of 700-800℃. A new achievement in colored porcelain, *doucai* first appeared in the Xuande period and was perfected during the Chenghua reign. The jar in the picture, an example of remarkable artistic craftsmanship, appears clear, bright and splendid. A book titled *Exploring the Works of Nature* gives a full account of porcelain making in the Ming Dynasty. An illustration from the book is reproduced here.

打圈

回青
畫

82. Covered jar with fish-and-alga design of the Jiajing period   Ornament, 46 cm high, 24.8 cm in diameter at the bottom, Ming Dynasty. This jar is decorated with pictures of plants and animals artistically arranged: lotus petals on the shoulders; fish, algae and lotus flowers on the upper belly; and banana leaves on the lower belly. On the bottom of the jar are six characters written in blue on a white background reading in translation, "Made in the Jiajing period of the Great Ming." The Ming Dynasty developed several varieties of porcelain: single-glaze, *doucai,* and five-color porcelain. Five-color articles made in the Jiajing reign were more beautiful than those from earlier periods. This type of porcelain, mostly with blue and white as the background color, is decorated with designs in red, yellow, blue, green or purple, but not necessarily all of them on the same piece. It was produced in a single or two firings. The jar in the picture, made in a single firing, is a gem of Ming colored porcelain.

83. Steel sword   Weapon, overall length 97.4 cm long, blade 79.2 cm long, hilt 18.2 cm long, sheath 83.2 cm long, Ming Dynasty. The Ming Dynasty saw rapid development of the iron-smelting industry. During the Hongwu reign (1368-1398) iron-smelting companies run by the government numbered 13. The iron-smelting company in Zunhua (now Zunhua County, Hebei Province), for instance, boasted a smelting furnace measuring over 6 m high, 4 m deep, more than 2 m in diameter inside, and more than 3 m in diameter outside. It produced not only pig iron but also wrought iron and steel. The government used steel primarily for making household utensils and weapons. The sword in the picture, a relic of the Ming Dynasty, is still sharp, pliable, and not too rusty, indicating the advanced technical level of the Ming Dynasty in steel-making.

83

84

84. Copper incense burner with cloud design of the Xuande period Ritual vessel, overall height 91.9 cm, Ming Dynasty. During the Ming Dynasty a large quantity of copper was produced to meet ever-increasing demands. On Wudang Mountain, Hubei Province, stands a copper structure, known as Golden Palace, built during the Yongle period. It is 5.54 m high, 3.15 m deep and 4.4 m wide, with structural members of prefabricated copper. In Beijing, a Ming copper bell in Juesheng Temple weighs 46.5 tons.During the Xuande period, Emperor Xuanzong, discovering that the ritual vessels in use did not conform to the ancient system, ordered the Board of Works to produce new ones for use in temples and ceremonies. In the course of production the Board of Works referred to Qin-Han ritual vessels and the Song porcelain made in the Guan, Ru, Ding and Ge kilns.

Copper incense burners made in the Xuande period were later referred to as Xuande burners. Cast in high quality copper, Xuande burners feature a simple and unsophisticated shape, a brown or purple color, and a beautiful inscription. The burner pictured bears an inscription meaning "Made in the Xuande period of the Great Ming."

Development of the Mercantile Economy

During the Ming Dynasty, as agriculture and the handicraft industry further developed, commerce flourished. Commercial cities and towns mushroomed, especially along the banks of the Yangtze River and the Grand Canal, where the commercial centers of Nanjing, Suzhou, Wuchang, Hangzhou and Linqing were situated. Small towns in the lower Yangtze valley also grew quickly; some, such as Shengze, Zhenze, Puyuan and Wangjiangjing, became textile trading centers. In the commercial cities and towns, large and small, people gathered from all quarters, coming to buy and sell all over the country. Changes were evident in the money supply in this mercantile economy. Early in the Ming Dynasty only paper money and copper coins were allowed to circulate; gold or silver transactions were prohibited. By the mid-Ming, with the enormous increase of money in circulation, gold and silver were widely used to facilitate trade. At the same time, the seeds of capitalism began to appear in the textile industry in the lower Yangtze valley. Some wealthy people bought looms and hired weavers to work for them; the weavers were paid daily wages. And, in the trade of Songjiang cloth, merchants with characteristics of capitalist contractors numbered in the hundreds.

85. Copper weight made in Yingtian Prefecture during the Jianwen period
Part of a Ming Dynasty weighing instrument, 5.5 cm high, 2.5 cm in diameter at the bottom. This was a sliding weight used on a steelyard, an indispensable instrument for commercial activities. The heavier the sliding weight, the greater the maximum amount that could be weighed with the steelyard. Weights were generally made of iron, copper or stone. The copper weight in the picture was made in 1399, the first year of the Jianwen reign, in Yingtian Prefecture (now Nanjing).

86. *Baochao* paper money Currency, 34.1 x 22.2 cm, Ming Dynasty. In 1375, the eighth year of the Hongwu reign, the Ming emperor Zhu Yuanzhang set up a bureau and ordered the printing of *baochao,* a form of paper money such as is depicted. The paper money, also known as Hongwu *baochao,* was printed on light greenish blue paper made of mulberry stalks. Across the top are six characters meaning "The *Baochao* of Great Ming for Circulation." Below them are "One *Guan*" and "Ten Strings of Copper Coins," flanked by "The *Baochao* of Great Ming" and "For Circulation Throughout the Land." On its lower part are sentences meaning "The *baochao* of Great Ming, printed by the Board of Revenue with His Majesty's permission, is to circulate together with copper coins. Whosoever forges *baochao* dies! ..." The frames on its four sides are decorated with images of the sea, dragons and intertwining branches. According to Ming government regulations, one *guan* was equal to ten strings of copper coins, or 1,000 *wen,* or a tael of silver, or a quarter of a tael of gold. Six kinds of *baochao* were issued during the Ming Dynasty, with face values 100, 200, 300, 400, and 500 *wen* and one *guan*. Because the use of silver was prohibited, the proliferation of *baochao* led to its rapid devaluation. Paper money was rarely seen by the middle of the 15th century and was officially withdrawn from circulation in 1522, the first year of the Jiajing reign.

85

87. "The Splendor of an Imperial Capital" (section of a long colored scroll on silk)
Whole scroll 32 x 2,182.6 cm, Ming Dynasty. The scroll depicts bustling Beijing when it served as the imperial capital during the mid-and late Ming Dynasty. Beginning from Marco Polo Bridge, we see the Gate of Universal Peace, which led to the city proper; the South-Facing Gate; Qipan Street; the Great Ming Gate; Chengtianmen (now Tian'anmen); the imperial palace; and, finally, Juyong Pass, an important fortification in the north for the protection of the capital. The artist's focus was on the capital's commercial districts with their jostling crowds, endless stream of horses and carriages, teahouses, wineshops, shops for gold and silver exchange, and the circus and street performers that attracted large audiences. The section pictured shows the busy scenes around the South-Facing Gate, Qipan Street and Great Ming Gate.

87-1

88. Small steelyard Weighing instrument, scaled arm 31.1 cm long, tray 8.5 cm in diameter, counterpoise 4.7 cm high and 94.6 g in weight, Ming Dynasty. The steelyard in the picture, called *dengzi* in Chinese, was for weighing precious goods such as gold, silver and medicines. The scaled arm, made of ivory, has two loops for suspending from the user's hand. The marks for the first loop range from 5 to 20 taels, and those for the second loop, from zero to 5 taels. The tray and the counterpoise, with the words "Made in the Wanli period" on the bottom, are made of gilded silver. A precise, exquisite instrument, the steelyard gives readings not only of tael but also weight of the *qian* (1 *qian* = 0.1 tael) and the *fen* (1 *fen* = 0.01 tael). Because paper money had been withdrawn from circulation and copper coins were too heavy, silver became a favorable medium of exchange, and small steelyards were ideal instruments for weighing silver, during the middle and late Ming Dynasty.

89. Ivory abacus Calculating instrument, 27.1 cm long, 15.2 cm wide, Ming Dynasty. An indispensable instrument for Ming Dynasty merchants and statisticians, the abacus consists of a rectangular frame and a long transverse bar dividing the frame into upper and lower parts. The frame holds parallel rods strung with two movable beads on the upper part and five on the lower part. Each of the beads on the upper part is equivalent to the five beads on the lower part of the same rod, and the beads on the rods are decimal from right to left. Mnemonic abacus rhymes popular in the Ming Dynasty are still used today. No conclusion has yet been reached as to when the abacus first appeared in China. Some say that it was already in use during the Yuan Dynasty, but no material evidence can be produced to prove this. It is certain, however, that the abacus was popular by the time of the Ming Dynasty, for the book *Systematic Treatise on Arithmetic,* written by Cheng Dawei during the Wanli reign of the Ming Dynasty, records abacus rhymes and illustrates an abacus that is identical to modern ones. The abacus pictured here was exquisitely made: its beads can be moved easily even today.

90. "Thriving Southern Capital" Painting on silk, 44 x 350 cm, Ming Dynasty. Nanjing (meaning "southern capital") became the capital when the Ming Dynasty was established under Zhu Yuanzhang. After the dynasty moved its capital to Beijing, a nominal central government still existed in Nanjing. The second largest city of the Ming Dynasty, Nanjing had good land and water transport facilities, advanced silk and cotton textile industries, and a flourishing mercantile economy. The painting vividly shows the prosperity of Nanjing at the time. Beginning with farmhouses in the suburbs, it centers in South and North Market Streets and ends at the imperial palace. From the painting we see a crosshatched pattern of streets, shops with colorful signboards, people, and horses and carriages. Altogether some 1,000 people of all occupations and 109 shops with their signboards are depicted, reflecting the economy and social life of the Ming Dynasty. The painting is attributed to Qiu Ying, a famous Ming artist, but, judging from the brushwork, it may not be his work.

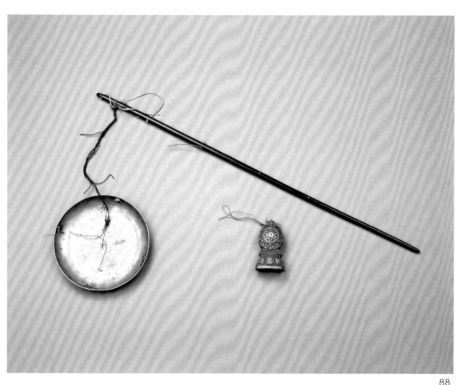

88

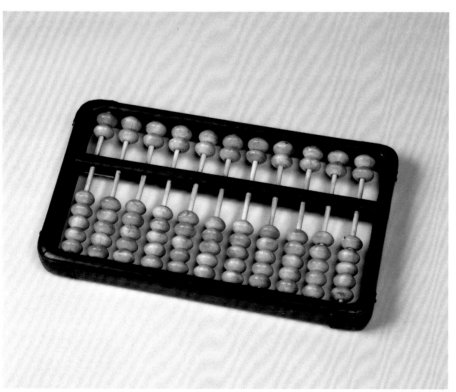

89

90-2

90-3

Social Life

The Ming Dynasty in its first years made radical changes in the dress, customs, ceremonies and etiquette of the Yuan Dynasty, its predecessor, with the result that a simple, honest mood prevailed. With economic development, cultural life became increasingly vibrant. Public places of amusement mushroomed in big cities, while in rural areas, operas were staged frequently. All religions, including Buddhism, Taoism and Islam, were protected by the government; festivals were celebrated in a more lively way than before. In the middle and late Ming Dynasty social life tended toward luxury, especially in dress; one after another, cases emerged of spending beyond the limit for clothing set by the government.

91. Cream-colored porcelain statue of Buddha Amitabha　Overall height 62.6 cm, Ming Dynasty. Buddha Amitabha, the founder of The Land of Ultimate Bliss in the west, is the principal divinity worshiped by the Pure Land Sect. The Buddha of Long Life, Amitabha is referred to by 13 names. He promises salvation to anyone who calls on his name with sincere devotion. In the picture Amitabha is portrayed wearing a kasaya, but is bare chested and barearmed; his hair is worn in a coil and his hands are folded in front of the abdomen. He sits crosslegged on a lotus throne, with eyes almost closed, looking kindly and affable. The atatue, dignified and elegant, brings the compassion of Amitabha to life. Most of the Ming emperors and their empresses and concubines were Buddhists or Taoists. Buddhist and Taoist temples could be found all over the country, with statues made of clay, wood or metal enshrined therein.

91-1

92-1

93. Copper burner and stand with Arabic inscriptions Overall height 22.3 cm, rim 24.1 cm in diameter, Ming Dynsaty. On the belly of the burner are two Arabic inscriptions meaning "Allah, the sole God" and "Mohammed, the chosen prophet of Allah," and on the bottom, six Chinese characters meaning "Made during the Zhende reign of the Great Ming." The stand is in the shape of lotus leaves. Because the Ming Dynasty adopted a policy of protection toward Islam, Muslims were able to participate in political activities and received many gifts from the government. The burner pictured was a gift to a mosque by the Ming government.

92. Blue and white gourd-shaped bottle with images of the Eight Immortals
Ornament, 58 cm high, 6.4 cm in diameter at the top and 19.2 at the bottom, Ming Dynasty. Ancient Chinese Taoists used the gourd as a vessel for holding water or medicine. The bottle in the picture features a small mouth, a contracted neck, a round upper part, and a four-sided lower part. The upper part is decorated with pictures of flying cranes and the Eight Trigrams formerly used in divination, and the lower part, with lifelike images of the Eight Immortals from Taoist mythology. Most emperors of the middle and late Ming Dynasty, especially Emperors Jiajing and Wanli, were devotees of Taoism. For this reason, many Ming vessels and textiles illustrate Taoist ideas.

93

94

94. "Emperor Xianzong with Birds"
Painting, 67 x 52.8 cm, Ming Dynasty. In
the painting, Emperor Xianzong (born Zhu
Jianshen) is depicted playing with birds
beneath two ancient trees in the imperial
garden. Wearing a civilian robe and cap,
the emperor points in amusement at birds
in a cage held by a eunuch, while another
younger eunuch follows behind.

**95. "Lantern Festival Celebrated in
Emperor Xianzong's Palace"** Scroll, 37 x

624 cm, Ming Dynasty. Emperor Xianzong,
with reign title Chenghua (1465-1487),
was the eighth monarch of the Ming
Dynasty. By his time the Ming government
had matured politically and achieved
great economic success after nearly a
hundred years of rule. At the same time,
however, various social contradictions
began to appear. Emperor Xianzong
ardently loved painting, but he was a
dissipated ruler with limited ability to

govern. The scroll pictured is a realistic
portrayal of the Lantern Festival
celebration in the imperial palace. It
depicts grand scenes of fireworks, lantern
displays, and performances of magic and
acrobatics, all observed by Emperor
Xianzong. The scroll is also an example of
Ming Dynasty genre painting. An
inscription in the scroll indicates that it
was done in the midwinter of the twenty-
first year of the Chenghua reign.

95-2

95-3

95-4

95-5

96. "Street Vendor" Genre painting, 190.6 x 104.5 cm, Ming Dynasty. In the painting we see a large open umbrella over a street vendor's cart, with specimens of small items suspended from the edge of the umbrella. Other small items for sale hang from four bamboo poles, and others are displayed here and there in the cart. Pushing the cart from street to street, the vendor beats a drum and gong to hawk his wares, and has attracted a large number of customers, old and young. Two small children are playing with toys they have bought, while the vendor busily deals with other customers. In the Ming Dynasty, street vendors were very active in both cities and the countryside.

97. Informal satin robe with cloud design Robe 128 cm long and 44 cm wide, sleeve 116 cm long, Ming Dynasty; unearthed in 1966 from the tomb of Wang Xijue in Suzhou, Jiangsu Province. Wang Xijue (1534-1610), a native of Taicang (now Taicang County, Jiangsu Province) was a high-ranking official in the Ming Dynasty cabinet. His body was so well preserved that, when it was unearthed, it seemed as if he had just died. Also unearthed from the tomb were 161 funerary objects, including hats, jade ornaments, furniture, and valuable silk and satin garments.

98-2

98. Empress Xiaojing's phoenix coronet
Relic of the Ming Dynasty, 27 cm high, rim 23.7 cm in diameter, weight 2,320 g; unearthed in 1957 from the Dingling tomb in Changping, Beijing. It was customary in the Ming Dynasty to bury the dead with full honors. The Ming emperor Wanli (reign 1573-1619) and two of his wives, Empresses Xiaoduan and Xiaojing, were buried in a tomb known as the Dingling in Bejijng. A total of 2,780 relics, including three phoenix coronets, were unearthed from the tomb. The phoenix coronet was a ceremonial headdress worn by an empress when she attended morning court, received a title bestowed by the emperor, or paid homage to the divinities at a temple. The coronet in the picture is lacquered bamboo on the inside and silk on the outside. A sumptuous headdress, it is decorated with nine gold dragons, nine gold phoenixes, about 5,000 pearls and nearly 100 rubies.

◁ 98-1

Foreign Relations

The Ming Dynasty, while maintaining close political and economic ties with various Asian countries, took active measures to establish good relations with other countries. Shortly after the founding of the dynasty, it had diplomatic relations with its neighbors, including Korea, Japan, Luzon and Siam. Trade and tributary relations were established with many Asian and African countries after Ming envoys visited them with offers of trade and friendship. Bureaus of Foreign Trade were set up in Guangzhou, Quanzhou and Ningbo to strengthen economic ties abroad. Zheng He, as an envoy of the Ming government, sailed to Southeast Asia and the Indian Ocean seven times, successfully carrying out his mission. During the late Ming Dynasty, the Ming government enhanced its relations with countries in Asia, Africa and Europe, while concentrating on battling Japanese pirates who were causing problems in the coastal areas. In the 16th century, with the eastward expansion of Western colonialism, the Chinese people were compelled to battle colonialism.

Zheng He Sails the "Western Oceans"

In the Ming Dynasty the sea area west of Kalimantan was referred to as the "Western Oceans" by the Chinese people. Between 1405, the third year of the Yongle reign, and 1433, the eighth year of the Xuande reign, when the nation's economy revived and expanded, Zheng He, as an envoy of the Ming Dynasty, led fleets of treasure-laden ships across the "Western Oceans" seven times, once traveling as far as the Red Sea and the eastern coast of Africa. On each voyage he took a fleet of over 100 ships (on one occasion, 208 ships) and an entourage of 28,000, including sailors, administrative officials, soldiers, technicians, interpreters, medical workers and handymen. Sixty-three of the ships constituted the main body of the fleet; the largest of these ships measured 148 meters long and 60 meters wide. Such spectacular voyages had never been undertaken before in recorded history. The seven expeditions led by Zheng He earned China international ronown, won the trust of Asian and African countries, and greatly strengthened China's economic and cultural ties with these countries. Massive quantities of China's silks and porcelains went to Asian and African countries, whereas Asian and African specialities were likewise imported into China in vast amounts. Zheng He, a Muslim, whose original name was Ma Sanbao, entered the palace as a eunuch during the Hongwu reign. The surname Zheng was bestowed on him by Emperor Yongle (born Zhu Di) because of his meritorious deeds in helping Zhu Di, then Prince of Yan, take the throne.

99

99. Zheng He's navigation map   This navigation map, made by Zheng He and others in Nanjing about the first year of the Xuande reign, was given a long title, namely "Map showing voyage of ships which set sail from the dockyard, put to sea at Longjiangguan and reached various foreign countries." Mao Yuanyi, a scholar of the Ming Dynasty, added it as appendix to his *Treatise on Armament Technology*. The ships, as shown on the map, set sail from Nanjing and reached as far as Mombasa, Kenya, on the east coast of Africa.The bearings of the countries along the shipping line, as well as the mileage, reefs and shoals, are all indicated. Also indicated are about 500 place names, including some 300 foreign names.

100. Zheng He's bronze bell   Overall height 83 cm, rim 49 cm in diameter, thickness 2 cm, weight 77 kg, Ming Dynasty. In 1431, the sixth year of the Xuande reign, Zheng He was ordered to set out on an expedition to the west for the seventh time. He first arrived in Changle, Fujian, in February, waiting for the winter monsoon to pass. In May, he sailed along the Min River to Nanpingzhen. While there, he and others ordered a bronze bell cast and gave it as alms to a temple; in this way they hoped and prayed for a safe journey across the "western oceans." He put to sea at Changle in November. The bell, as shown in the picture, has a sunflower-shaped mouth and a handle decorated with two coiled dragons. Engraved on the upper part of its belly are eight characters meaning "The elements are propitious, the country prospers and the people live at peace," and, on the lower part, a long sentence stating when and why Zheng He and others had the bell cast.

100

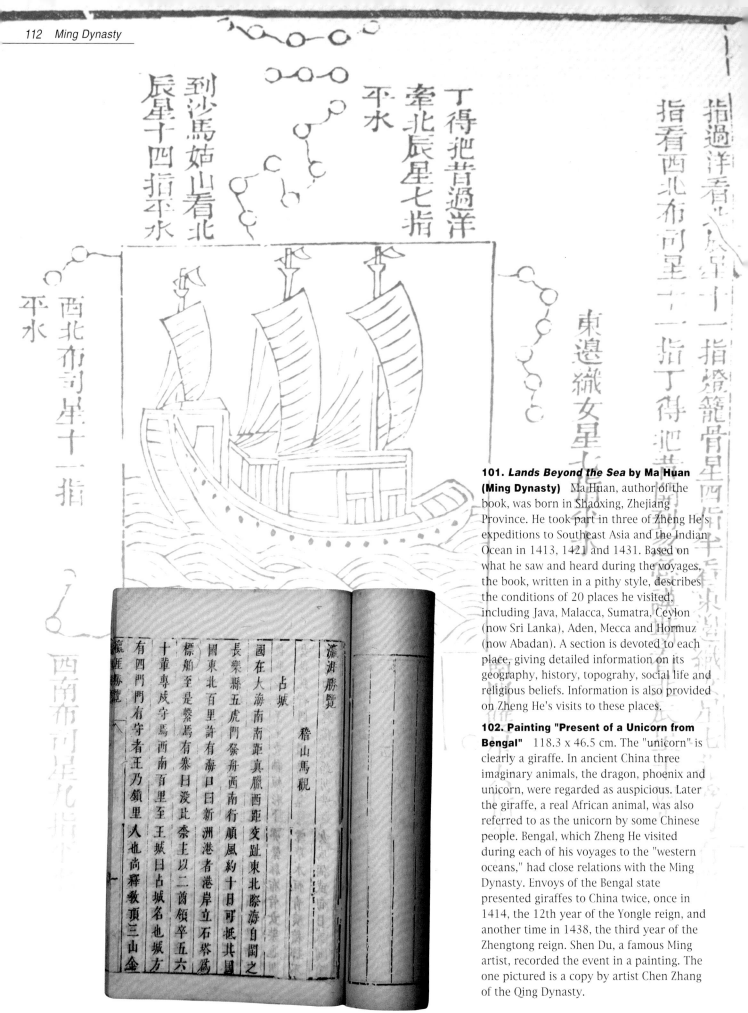

平水

西北布司星十一指

到沙馬姑山看北
辰星十四指平水

牽北辰星七指
平水

丁得把昔過洋

平水

指過洋看

指看西北布司星十一指丁得把昔

東邊織女星

西南布司星九指

101. *Lands Beyond the Sea* by Ma Huan (Ming Dynasty) Ma Huan, author of the book, was born in Shaoxing, Zhejiang Province. He took part in three of Zheng He's expeditions to Southeast Asia and the Indian Ocean in 1413, 1421 and 1431. Based on what he saw and heard during the voyages, the book, written in a pithy style, describes the conditions of 20 places he visited, including Java, Malacca, Sumatra, Ceylon (now Sri Lanka), Aden, Mecca and Hormuz (now Abadan). A section is devoted to each place, giving detailed information on its geography, history, topograhy, social life and religious beliefs. Information is also provided on Zheng He's visits to these places.

102. Painting "Present of a Unicorn from Bengal" 118.3 x 46.5 cm. The "unicorn" is clearly a giraffe. In ancient China three imaginary animals, the dragon, phoenix and unicorn, were regarded as auspicious. Later the giraffe, a real African animal, was also referred to as the unicorn by some Chinese people. Bengal, which Zheng He visited during each of his voyages to the "western oceans," had close relations with the Ming Dynasty. Envoys of the Bengal state presented giraffes to China twice, once in 1414, the 12th year of the Yongle reign, and another time in 1438, the third year of the Zhengtong reign. Shen Du, a famous Ming artist, recorded the event in a painting. The one pictured is a copy by artist Chen Zhang of the Qing Dynasty.

瀛涯勝覽

稽山馬觀

占城

國在大海南南距真臘西距
交趾東北際海自閩之
長樂縣五虎門發舟西南行順風約
十日可抵其國
國東北百里許有海口曰新
洲港者港岸立石塔為
標船至是繫焉有番曰沒此
奈主以二商領卒五六
十輩專戍守焉西南百里至
王城曰占城名也城方
有四門門有守者王乃領里
人也尚釋教頂三山金

瀛涯勝覽【一】

按一統志玉斫續文獻通考榜葛剌即東印度也國最大從蘇門答剌海
西行二十日抵溜洄地港至璜納見江有城池街市聚貨通市直行至㭪歇
噎酋長居馬城廊甚嚴其國殿宇廣大門內三重九間殿柱皆黃銅色飾
雕琢花為左右長廊內設明甲馬隊千餘外列巨漢甲冑執鋒叉弓矢舟
埤左右列孔雀銅扇蓋數百又置象隊王正殿高座嵌八寶王箕踞坐其上
橫銅於膝王及諸官皆回之男祝髮白布纏頭圓領長衣束綠悅驒金錦
羊皮犖婦人不范胎粉耳垂寶銅項掛纓絡
永樂六年榜葛刺國王霭牙思遠使来貢至正統後不復至

和露文文大人補壁即請　　正腕

菊泉璋 [印]

臨為

The Ming Empire's Relations with Japan and Korea

Diplomatic and trade relations were established between China and Japan after the founding of the Ming Dynasty. A problem, however, was created by Japanese pirates, who raided and pillaged Chinese coastal areas early in the Ming Dynasty and stepped up their lawless activities along China's southeastern coast in the middle Ming period. Chinese soldiers and civilians, led by Qi Jiguang and Yu Dayou, rose against the invaders and thoroughly ousted them late in the Jiajing reign after fighting nearly a hundred bloody battles in the coastal areas of Jiangsu, Zhejiang, Fujian and Guangdong.

The Ming empire had a close relationship with Korea. In the late 16th century Japan adopted an expansionist foreign policy and twice attempted to conquer Korea. At the request of the king of Korea, the Ming government sent troops to join the Korean army in driving Japanese invaders out.

103

104-1

103. Large Japanese bronze mirror Rim
76.5 cm in diameter, weight 46.25 kg, Edo
period of Japan; unearthed in 1947 at
Kaiyuan Temple, Quanzhou, Fujian
Province. This bronze mirror, made in
Japan during the Edo period, entered
China in the late Ming Dynasty, delivered
to Quanzhou by a Japanese merchant ship
and presented as an offering to the
Kaiyuan Temple. Together with Ningbo
and Guangzhou, Quanzhou was one of the
three ports where a bureau in charge of
foreign trade was set up during the Ming
Dynasty.

**104. Blue and white incense burner
made by Goryo Oura (Wu Xiangrui) with
birds, flowers and human figures** 16th-
century product of Japan, overall height
14.2 cm, rim 8.2 cm in diameter. This

incense burner features a round mouth, a
pierced lid, a knob decorated with the
image of a reclining lion, and a hexagonal
body with paintings of birds, flowers and
human figures on the six sides. The
human figures, wearing long, loose, wide-
sleeved robes, are painted in a distinctive
Japanese style. On the bottom of the
burner are the words "Made by Goryo
Oura (Wu Xiangrui)" written in blue.
Goryo Oura, who took the Chinese name
of Wu Xiangrui, was born in Ise Matsunra.
In the early 16th century he was taken to
China along with Ryoan, a Japanese monk,
to learn porcelain-making. After returning
to Japan in 1513, he set up a kiln for
making blue-and-white porcelain near
Arida, Hida, ushering in a porcelain boom
in Japan. As a pioneer of Japanese

porcelain, he did not strictly adhere to the
Chinese methods for producing blue-and-
white porcelain, but introduced
innovations. "Arida porcelain" is still a
famous brand in Japan today.

104-2

105. Qi Jiguang's saber Weapon, overall length 89 cm, length of handle 16 cm, Ming Dynasty. Qi Jiguang (1528-1587), a native of Dongmou, Shandong, inherited an official title in Dengzhou. Later, he was appointed lieutenant colonel of Zhejiang and, together with the army led by Yu Dayou, put down the Japanese pirates in Zhejiang and Fujian. After that he led his troops southward to Guangdong and routed the Japanese pirates along China's southeastern coast. In 1568, the second year of the Longqing reign, Qi Jiguang was transferred to the north as a garrison commander in Jizhou. He held the office for 16 years, during which he directed the construction of many defense fortifications in the north, including the extant Ming Great Wall. The saber in the picture has an inscription indicating that it was cast in 1582, the 10th year of the Wanli reign, when Qi Jiguang served his tenure of office in Jizhou.

105-2

105-1

106-1

106. Scroll painting "Fighting the Japanese Pirates" (section) Colored painting on silk, complete scroll 31.1 x 572.7 cm, Ming Dynasty. This is a historical scroll depicting the battle between Zhejiang soldiers and civilians and Japanese pirates along China's coast during the Jiajing reign (1522-1566) of the Ming Dynasty. Beginning with the pirates' ships appearing on the horizon, the scroll consists of these sections:

"Landing of Japanese Pirates," "Burning, Killing and Pillaging," "People Take Refuge," "The Ming Army Goes Into Battle," "Fierce Fighting on the Sea," "Japanese Pirates Annihilated," and "Report of Victory." The sections pictured are "Fierce Fighting on the Sea" and "Report of Victory." A similar Ming scroll depicting the combat against Japanese pirates is now kept in Kyoto University, Japan.

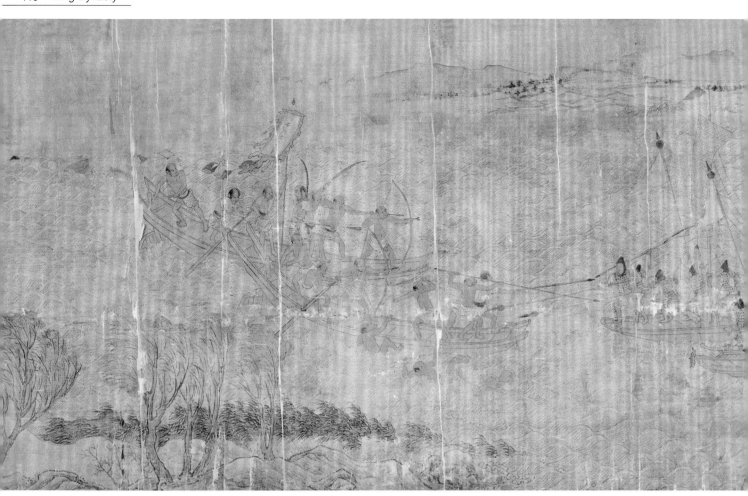

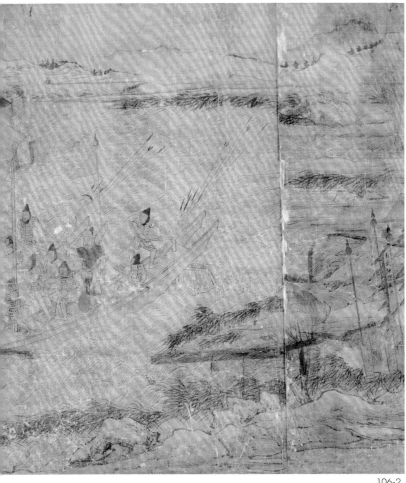

106-2

106-3

107. Folding fan   Korean artifact. In 1597 Toyotomi Hideyoshi of Japan launched a second war of aggression against Korea. By order of the Ming government, Xing Jie, minister of the Board of War, led an army to fight the Japanese invaders in Korea. While there, he was befriended by many Koreans. The folding fan pictured was one of the gifts Xing Jie received when he left Korea for home. The folding fan is said to have originated in Korea. Korean fans are exquisitely made and wear well.

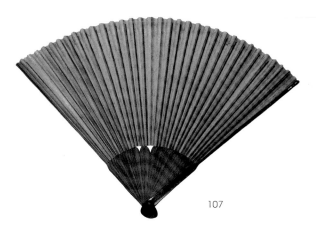

107

Science and Culture

The Ming Dynasty saw new achievements in science and technology, art, literature, and philosophy. A number of outstanding scientists, philosophers, artists and men of letters emerged and, with their works of timeless value, enriched the treasure-house of ancient Chinese science and culture. The Ming empire also made efforts to systematize ancient books and records, resulting in *The Yongle Encyclopaedia.*

Science and Technology

A number of illustrious scientists, namely Li Shizhen, Xu Xiake, Xu Guangqi and Song Yingxing, were active during the Ming Dynasty. These scientists and their works, *Compendium of Materia Medica, Travels of Xu Xiake, Exploiting the Works of Nature* and *A Complete Treatise on Agriculture,* hold important places in the history of Chinese science and technology.

108. *Exploiting the Works of Nature* by Song Yingxing Song Yingxing (1587-?), a native of Fengxin, Jiangxi Province, was an outstanding scientist in the late Ming Dynasty. He held a number of official provincial posts in Jiangxi and Fujian, but later resigned and returned to his home in the countryside. His *Exploiting the Works of Nature,* a famous scientific work in 18 volumes, was first published in 1637, the 10th year of the Chongzhen reign. It records the process of production and experience in agriculture and sidelines at the time, such as the use of bone ash in the fields, the earliest recorded use of phosphate fertilizer in agriculture, and the theory that "plants differ according to the local environment," which provided the theoretical basis for cultivating improved seeds. Also recorded in the book are the achievements of ancient Chinese handicraft industry, such as the jacquard loom, which turned out elegant, exquisitely patterned silk fabrics; the building of boats and vehicles; and the mining, smelting and founding of metals. The record of zinc-smelting technology is the earliest in the world. This book, richly illustrated, is a highly valuable contribution to the history of ancient science and technology. Thirteen illustrations from the book are shown here: 108-1 Smelting copper; 108-2 Making bell molds and casting *fu* (a caldron used in ancient China); 108-3 Casting *ding* (ancient Chinese cooking vessel); 108-4 Forging anchors; 108-5 Making bows and arrows; 108-6 Brick-making; 108-7 Jacquard loom; 108-8 Paper-making; 108-9 Making ink sticks; 108-10 Mining for silver; 108-11 Coal mining in south China; 108-12 Searching for jade; 108-13 Searching in water for pearls.

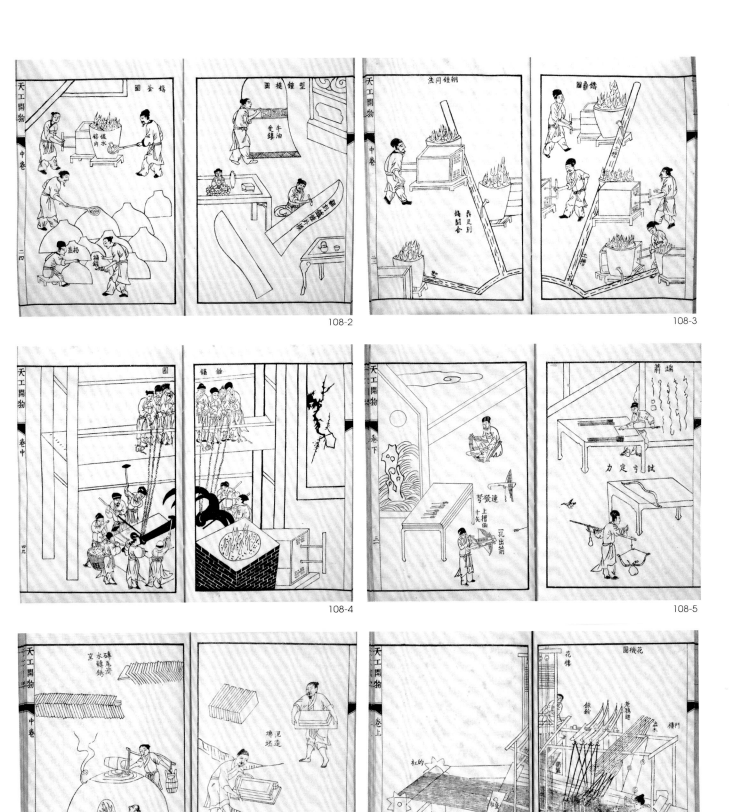

108-2

108-3

108-4

108-5

108-6

108-7

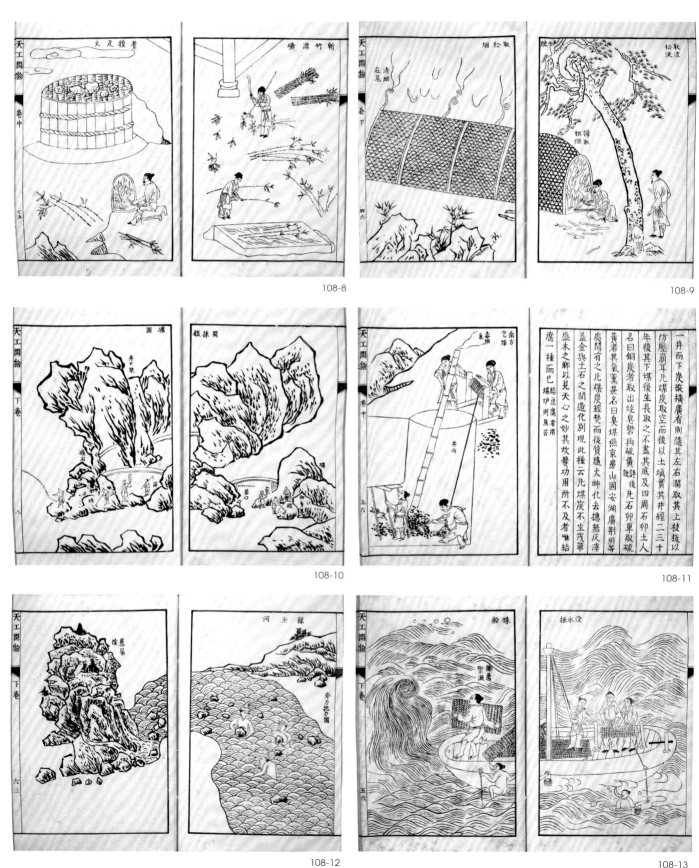

108-8

108-9

108-10

108-11

108-12

108-13

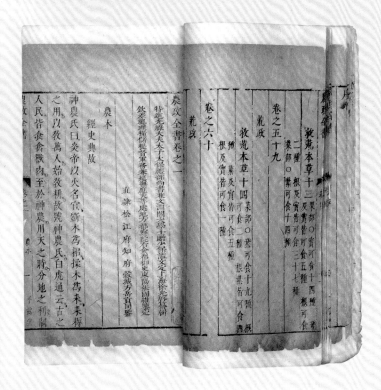

109.

109. A Complete Treatise on Agriculture by Xu Guangqi   Xu Guangqi (1562-1633), a native of Shanghai, passed the highest imperial examinations in 1604, the 32nd year of the Wanli reign, and became a *daxueshi,* a high-ranking official responsible for drafting imperial edicts. He excelled in many branches of learning, especially agriculture and astronomy. His *Complete Treatise on Agriculture,* an important work of over 500,000 words, divides into 12 *damu* and 60 *juan.* The part titled *Nongben* contains quotations from classics and exponents of various schools concerning agricultural production and policies. *Tianzhi* recounts the land system research made by the author and other ancient Chinese agronomists. *Nongshi* sums up ancient Chinese farming methods and knowledge of weather during the growing season. *Nongqi,* a richly illustrated section, describes traditional Chinese farm tools and tools for processing farm produce. *Huangzheng* summarizes policies on famine relief implemented in various historical periods and explains the benefits of wild plants.

110. Travels of Xu Xiake by Xu Xiake
Xu Xiake (1587-1641), a native of Jiangyin in what is now Jiangsu Province, was a well-known geographer and traveler in the Ming Dynasty. From age twenty-two, until the year before he died, he traveled across the length and breadth of China, leaving his footprints in what are now the 16 provinces of Jiangsu, Zhejiang, Anhui, Fujian, Guangdong, Guangxi, Jiangxi, Henan, Shanxi, Shandong, Hebei, Shaanxi, Hunan, Hubei, Guizhou and Yunnan. Wherever he visited, he made a careful survey and recorded the topography, geology, vegetation, climate and hydrological conditions, compiling this into *Travels of Xu Xiake.* The *Travels* provides a minute description of the karst landscape in China's southwest, the earliest known description of such topography. It correctly records the origins and courses of the Pan, Nu, Lancang and Red rivers, and points out that the Jinsha River constitutes the upper reach of the Yangtze.

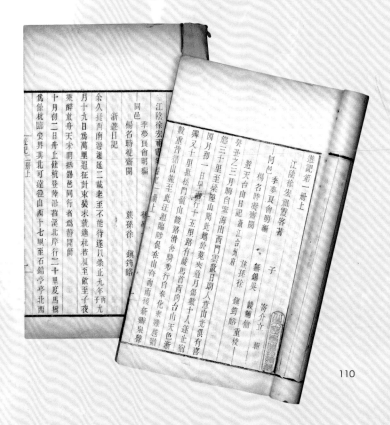

110

111

111. *Compendium of Materia Medica* by Li Shizhen

Li Shizhen (1518-1593), a native of Qizhou (now Qichun, Hubei Province), carried on his father's profession of physician in the Ming Dynasty. His *Compendium of Materia Medica* is a monumental book of over 1.9 million words on Chinses medicine and pharmacology, which greatly contributed to the systematic study of botany. He began writing it in 1552, the 31st year of the Jiajing reign, and finished 26 years later, in 1578, the sixth year of the Wanli reign. In the course of writing the book, he consulted over 800 medical books, and drew on his own experiences. He revised the text three times. Divided into 16 *bu,* 62 *lei* and 50 *juan,* the book describes 1,892 species of drugs—animal, vegetable and mineral substances—and includes 11,096 prescriptions and 1,100 illustrations. The drugs are classified scientifically. For instance, animal-based drugs are divided into *chong* (insect), *lin* (fish), *jie* (mollusk) and *qin* (bird).

112. Medicine cabinet lacquered in black with dragon design traced in gold

Medical article, 94.1 cm high, 78.9 cm long, 57 cm wide, Ming Dynasty. This cabinet, used in the imperial dispensary, has two doors and four legs with copper feet. Coated with black lacquer, the front and the two sides of the cabinet are decorated with dragon designs traced in gold; the back and the insides of the two doors are covered with flower-and-butterfly designs, also traced in gold. Inside are 80 drawers each of which stored one species of drug. In each of the two sides are ten long drawers, each divided into three compartments, for storing three separate kinds of drug. Thus the cabinet can hold 140 species of drugs, and the names of drugs are written in Chinese ink on the drawers. At the bottom of the cabinet are three large drawers for storing prescriptions and various medical articles, and on its back, an inscription in gold which reads in translation, "Made in the Wanli reign of the Great Ming."

112-1

112-2 ▷

Philosophy

The philosophy before the mid-Ming Dynasty mainly borrowed and developed the Neo-Confucianism of the Song Dynasty. Neo-Confucianism is an idealistic ideology characterized by a blending of Confucianism, Taoism and Buddhism with Confucianism at the heart. Its objective idealism was represented by the two Chengs (namely, Cheng Hao and Cheng Yi) and Zhu Xi of the Song Dynasty, and its subjective idealism was represented by Lu Jiuyuan of the Song Dynasty. In the early days of the Ming Dynasty, the Neo-Confucianism of the two Chengs and Zhu was in vogue; after mid-Ming, Wang Shouren (Wang Yangming) developed the Neo-Confucianist thinking of Lu Jiuyuan and founded the Wang school of philosophy. At the end of the Ming, thinker Li Zhi opposed the Neo-Confucianism of the Song and Ming dynasties.

113. Portrait of Wang Shouren Wang Shouren (1472-1529), courtesy name Bo'an, from Yuyao (in present-day Zhejiang Province), well-known philosopher in the Ming Dynasty. As he had once studied in the Yangming Cave in Shaoxing, Zhejiang, he was known as Master Yangming. He borrowed the Neo-Confucianism of Lu Jiuyuan of the Song Dynasty, and advocated "The Theory of Innate Knowledge", also known as the "Wang school of philosophy," which stressed "there is nothing outside the mind." He gathered his followers and lectured to them in Guizhou, Jiangxi and Zhejiang. His followers later compiled his writings into the *Complete Book of Master Wang Yangming,* altogether 38 volumes, among which the *Record of Great Learning* was his main philosophical treatise.

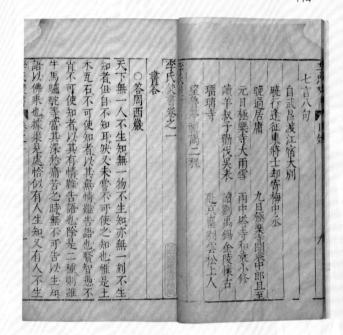

114

113

114. *Book Burning* Written by Li Zhi. Li Zhi (1527-1602), courtesy name Zhuo'wu, from Jinjiang County, Fujian Province, an anti-feudal enlightenment thinker of the Ming Dynasty. He passed the imperial examination at the provincial level when he was 26 and served as a junior official for many years. He resigned in his old age and took up writing and lecturing. He sharply criticized the Neo-Confucianism of the Song and Ming dynasties, opposed the asceticism of Neo-Confucianists of suppressing "human desires" with "heavenly principles," put forward the idea that "attire and eating are human" and stressed the importance of material life. The *Book Burning* was one of his main works, completed in 1590, the 18th year of the Wanli reign of the Ming Dynasty. After publishing *Book Burning,* he explained to those who came to hear his lecture that because the book included contents contrary to the ethics advocated by the rulers, he chose the name *Book Burning* to show his lack of fear. Preferring to die rather than give up his ideas, Li Zhi committed suicide in prison in 1602, the 30th year of the Wanli reign, at the age of 76.

Novels, Traditional Opera, Music and Reference Books

In the Ming Dynasty, a number of outstanding novels appeared such as the *Romance of The Three Kingdoms* written by Luo Guanzhong, *Outlaws of the Marsh* written by Shi Nai'an, *Journey to the West* written by Wu Cheng' en, and a number of literary works reflecting daily life of ordinary people in the Ming Dynasty, certain achievements were also scored in the fields of traditional opera and music. The Ming government also organized the compilation of the voluminous reference book, the *Yongle Encyclopedia*.

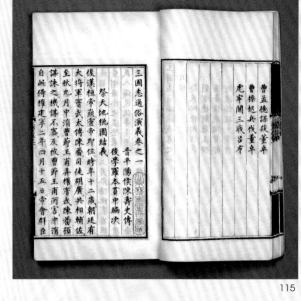

115

115. *Romance of the Three Kingdoms*

Written by Luo Guanzhong, a novelist towards the end of the Yuan Dynasty and the beginning of the Ming Dynasty. Taking the political and military struggles during the Three Kingdoms Period as the theme, he wrote this novel, grand in composition, intricate in plot and comprising a wide variety of characteristics. This highly influential novel served as a textbook in the fields of history and military affairs, and established the historical romance as literature, influencing later works. The most widely circulated version of the Romance of the Three Kingdoms is the revised edition from the early Qing Dynasty.

116. Part of scroll depicting figures in *Outlaws of the Marsh,* painted by Chen Laolian An imitation by a Qing Dynasty painter; the entire scroll is 20 cm long, 562.3 cm wide. *The Outlaws of the Marsh* is a novel based on a peasant uprising led by Song Jiang in the last years of the Northern Song Dynasty. The story of this uprising had spread among the people since the Southern Song Dynasty. From this popular folk legend, Shi Nai'an, who lived towards the end of the Yuan and the beginning of the Ming, revised the story

and wrote his novel, the *Outlaws of the Marsh*. Chen Laolian, a noted painter at the end of Ming and in early Qing, executed portraits of the figures described in the *Outlaws of the Marsh,* and an unknown painter of the Qing Dynasty then imitated Chen Laolian, depicting 40 high-ranking military leaders of the rebel army, with the name of each of them written in seal characters on the upper left, prefixed by a nickname. The figures shown in the picture are Song Jiang and Li Kui.

116-1

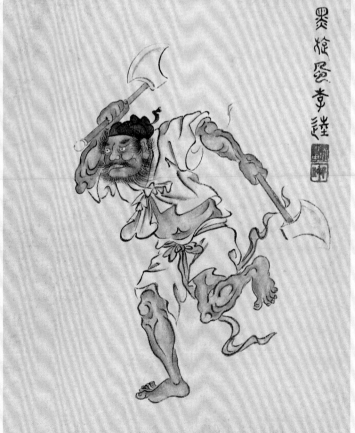

116-2

117-2

117-3

117. Chen Yixi annotated the *Journey to the West* album of illustrations *Journey to the West* is a full-length mythological novel describing how the Monkey King protected and escorted the Monk of Tang to India to obtain Buddhist scriptures, subduing demons and evil spirits and overcoming difficulties all along the way. The pilgrimage of Xuan Zang, an eminent Tang-dynasty monk, to India to obtain Buddhist scriptures is an actual historical event. After the Song Dynasty, the story was often told and it became a legend with a mythological flavor. Eventually, Ming-dynasty novelist Wu Chengen embellished the story, writing the *Journey to the West*. The Monkey King portrayed in the novel is brave, sagacious, dauntless and abhors evils. The portrayal of the monk of Tang and the Pig Deity is vivid. In the album of illustration of the *Journey to the West* Chen Yixi paired the images with simple language to carry the plot. Chen Yixi (1648-1709), from Haining (present-day Haining County, Zhejiang Province), was an excellent poet and calligrapher.

118-1

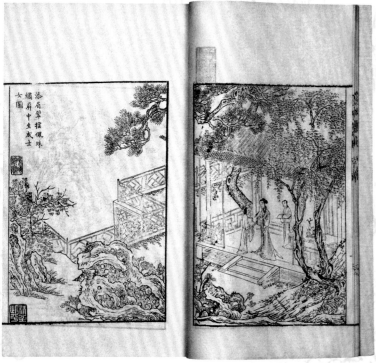

118-2

118. Portrait of Tang Xianzu and *Peony Pavilion* Tang Xianzu(1550-1616), courtesy name Yireng, from Linchuan (present-day Linchuan County, Jiangxi Province), was an outstanding literatus and dramatist of the Ming Dynasty born into a scholarly family. He was well-known for his talent in his early days and his main creative achievements were in traditional opera. His drama *Purple Hairpin, Peony Pavilion* (also known as *Soul Returns*), *The Southern Tributary State* and the *Dream of Handan* have been called the "four dreams of Linchuan", among which the *Peony Pavilion* is the longest, comprising 55 acts, depicting the love affair of Du Liniang and Liu Mengmei. Renowned for its beautiful language, it is his representative work. All embody the author's ideological inclination for the liberation of individual character and the yearning for the freedom in marriage.

119

119. Yongle Encyclopedia *Yongle Encyclopedia* is a reference book containing extracts from various books, compiled and classified according to the contents for the purpose of reference. *Yongle Encyclopedia* comprises 22,937 volumes in 11,095 copies, and preserves a large number of books and records. The book was completed in 1407, the 5th year of the Yongle reign, under the direction of Xie Jin, an academician of the Imperial Academy, and was named the *Yongle Encyclopedia* by Emperor Yongle. During the Jiajing reign, a copy was made, and the original was housed in the Chamber of the Source of Literature and the copy in the Imperial Library. At the end of the Ming Dynasty, the Chamber of the Source of Literature was burnt and the Yongle Encyclopedia which it held was lost; the other copy was either burnt or plundered during the invasion of Beijing by the Eight-power Allied Forces in 1900. Today only some 200 of the original 11,095 copies can be found in China.

120. Prince Lu's *zhong* he lute Ming Dynasty; stringed instrument; length 120 cm, width 19 cm. On the back of the lute are carved two Chinese characters "*zhong he*" in regular script, meaning the golden mean and harmony, the ideal state of Chinese classical aesthetics. On the belly of the lute are carved a poem and the name of the author: "The water of Yangtze reflects the moon, Dew drops glitter in a gentle breeze; When all is silent, Sentiments swell for remote antiquity. Master Jing Yi." On the tail of the lute is a seal bearing the Chinese characters in seal character, meaning "handed down from Prince Lu". Master Jing Yi was the courtesy name of Zhu Changfang, Prince Lu of the Ming Dynasty. He inherited the title of his father Zhu Yiliu in 1614, the 42nd year of the Wanli reign, and his feoffment was in the present-day Ji County, Henan Province. An achievement in music in the Ming Dynasty was the discovery of "twelve-tone equal temperament" by Zhu Zaiyu. The theory of "twelve-tone equal temperament" was expounded in details in his *Complete Book on Temperament*. The book also records folk songs and folk dances popular then, and expounds on the art of singing and of playing musical instruments.

120-1

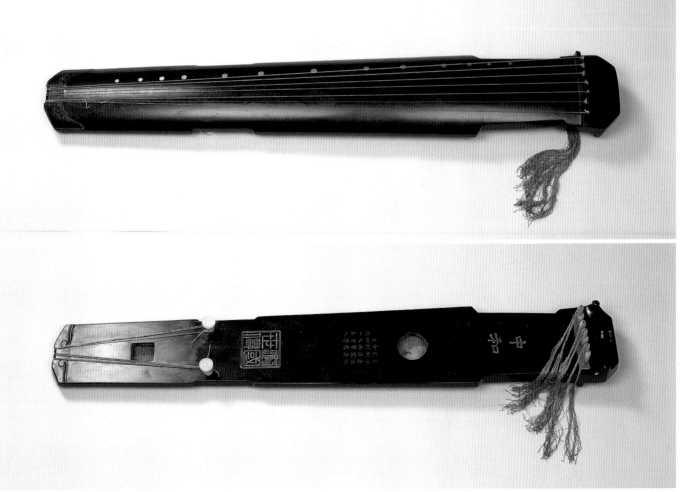

120-2

Handicraft and Painting

In the Ming Dynasty, cloisonné reached a high level and is representative of the dynasty. In addition, jadeware, bamboo carving and wood carving were very exquisite.

There were numerous schools of painting in the Ming Dynasty. One representative of the "imperial-court decorative painting" was Dai Jin. The practice of painting by literati in the Ming Dynasty was begun by Shen Zhou, Wen Zhengming, and Tang Yin, representatives of the Suzhou painting school; representative of splash-ink freehand brushwork painters was Xu Wei; among landscape painters, Dong Qichang had the greatest influence; the figure paintings of Chen Hongshou and Cui Zizhong were highly creative and the two were called "Chen of the south and Cui of the north".

Woodcuts in the Ming Dynasty were outstanding as well, and the *Ten-Bamboo Studio Painters' Manual* during the Tianqi reign was influential.

121. Filigree (Cloisonné) enamel pedestal bowl with fish and seaweed pattern Ming Dynasty; furnishing; 10.4 cm high, 14.9 cm in rim diameter, 4 cm in foot diameter. This is a flared-mouth pedestal bowl with white background inside, decorated with a fish and seaweed pattern, and sky blue background outside, decorated with passionflower pattern. Cloisonné enamel wares were made by welding thin copper wire onto a metallic body to form patterns, then filling in the spaces with various kinds of colored enamel glaze, firing under a high temperature, and finally polishing them. Cloisonné skill reached perfection during the period 1450-1456 in the Jingtai reign of the Ming Dynasty. The finished products had a predominantly blue background, appearing glittering and lustrous. It was also known as Jingtai Blue (cloisonné).

122-1

122. Carved red rectangular box with flower and bird pattern Ming Dynasty; length 36.7 cm, width 22 cm, height 11.3 cm. Carved red is a kind of carved lacquerware. In making carved lacquerware, lacquer is applied repeatedly on the surface, in as many as 30 layers. Then a design is carved into the thick lacquer. In this process, when red lacquer is used, it is called "carved red", and when yellow lacquer is used, "carved yellow". The skill of carving lacquerware was in vogue as early as the Song and Yuan dynasties, and by the time of the Ming Dynasty, the carved lacquerware skill far exceeded the previous dynasties. This carved red rectangular box is exquisite in craftsmanship, bright red in color, and of practical use as well as decoration. It is a superb example.

122-2

123-1

123. Black lacquer ewer inlaid with mother-of-pearl, made by Jiang Qianli Ming Dynasty; height 35 cm, width of mouth 6.3 cm, length 7 cm. The ewer was made by applying black lacquer on a rectangular tin body with a lid. There is space left on the four sides for inlays of red agate, coral, turquoise and mother-of-pearl, forming an exquisite pattern of flower, bird, butterfly and plum blossom. On the bottom of the foot are two Chinese characters, "Qianli", in seal character, inlaid with mother-of-pearl. Jiang Qianli was a noted craftsman of lacquerware inlay, long living in Yangzhou. As not many of his works were handed down to posterity, this ewer is priceless.

123-2

123-3 ▷

124-1

124. Palm, Rock and Crane A painting by Lu Ji; length 166.2 cm, width 106 cm; colored silk scroll. Lu Ji (1477-?), courtesy name Tingzhen, styled Leyu, from Yin County (present-day Ningbo, Zhejiang Province). An important court painter in the Ming Dynasty, he served in Renzhi Palace as commander of the imperial guard. He was a skilled flower-and-bird painter and copied the style of imperial-court decorative painting of the Northern and Southern Song dynasties. He was versed both in meticulous style painting in deep colors and in ink-and-wash freehand brushwork. Meticulously done, this painting, "Palm, Rock and Crane", is vivid and fully reflects the painting style of Lu Ji.

125. Sleeping Rock and Old Plum
Painted by Chen Hongshou; length 74.5 cm, width 43.5 cm. Chen Hongshou (1598-1652), courtesy name Zhanghou, styled Laolian, from Zhuji (in present-day Zhejiang Province), a renowned painter at the end of Ming and the beginning of the Qing Dynasty. After the decline of the Ming, to avoid Qing troops, he renounced his family and became a monk, styling himself Huichi and Laochi. He was skilled at painting the human figure, flower-and-bird designs as well as at a unique style of landscape painting. His painting had the appeal of hauteur and primitiveness, and had considerable influence upon later artists. In this painting, a huge rock lies horizontally across the bottom, beside it is an old plum tree with a bent and crooked trunk, and fresh and sturdy branches laden with clusters of plum blossoms. The picture was marvellously conceived, fresh and refined, having a sophisticated charm. On the upper right side of the picture, is inscribed "Chen Hongshou... Done in a tranquil residence."

125

Decline of the Ming Dynasty

In the middle Ming period, the annexation of land was very intense, as nobility, bureaucrats, the wealthy, kinsmen of the royal family and eunuchs plundered the land of the peasantry on a massive scale. Following the later middle Ming period, most emperors were incompetent, dissolute, superstitious or seeking immortality in odd ways while paying scant attention to state affairs for long periods. During the period from the rule of Emperor Yingzong to Emperor Wuzong of the Ming Dynasty, the arrogation of powers by eunuchs increased; during the rule of Emperor Shizong to the first years of Emperor Shenzong, powerful ministers held sway; and during the period from when Emperor Shenzong assumed the reins of government until the time of Emperor Xizong, the arrogation of power by eunuchs reached its peak in the Ming Dynasty. The eunuchs represented by Wei Zhongxian were denounced as "the eunuch clique." They held the emperor under their thumb and persecuted persons of integrity who dared to resist them. In the time of Wanli, the Manchus rose in northeast China and peasant uprisings occurred in succession. To raise money for war, the government constantly increased taxation, resulting in unbearably heavy burdens upon the peasantry. Beginning from the uprising of Wang Er, a peasant in Shaanxi, in 1627, the 7th year of the Tianqi reign, the rule of the Ming court faced overall collapse.

Political Crisis in the Later Ming Period

After the later mid-Ming period, emperors ignored state affairs, powerful ministers and eunuchs seized control, and the crisis in rule worsened. At the end of the 16th century, politician Zhang Juzheng strongly advocated reform, including a nation-wide measurement of land, introducing a single tax in silver, bringing floods under control, improving relations with the Mongolians and strengthening the defenses in the north. After the death of Zhang Juzheng, the political crisis of the Ming Dynasty was exacerbated. The struggle between the Donglin Faction and the eunuch clique heated up, and domestic troubles and foreign invasions pushed the autocracy of the Ming Dynasty to its last days.

126

126. Wooden seal of *jin yi wei* (imperial guards) Ming Dynasty seal made of wood; each side of seal-face 11.5 cm wide, seal-face1 cm thick, overall height 4 cm. The seal has contracted shoulders, a flat knob and some cracks. On the seal-face are carved Chinese characters *"jin yi wei"* in seal character, and, on its back, characters meaning "made by the three judicial organs in the 14th year (1478) of the Chenghua reign". *Jin yi wei* was an intelligence-gathering entity of the Ming Dynasty, set up in 1382, the 15th year of the Hongwu reign. It specialized in arrest, punishment and imprisonment and also was the emperor's bodyguard. The *jin yi wei* existed throughout the Ming Dynasty. In the beginning of the Ming Dynasty, to centralize authority, Zhu Yuanzhang set up the Board of Punishments, the Court of Censors and the Board of Justice to be in charge separately for criminal affairs; called all three judicial organs, and set them to restrain each other. In the time of important cases, the three would conduct a joint trial. The wooden seal was jointly carved by the three entities.

127-2

127. Bronze warrior plate in Leopard House Ming Dynasty; 9.8 cm high, 0.7 cm thick . A squatting leopard was cast on one side of the bronze plate and above it a horizontal line of Chinese characters cast which reads in translation "Leopard No. 1104". On the other side of the plate was cast "This plate is to be carried by a government warrior who keeps leopards; one who fails to carry the plate will be held guilty, so will be one who lends or borrows the plate." In the Ming Dynasty there was a Tiger House to the northwest of the Celestial Lake (present-day Central-South Lake and North Lake-Beihai), for keeping tigers. Zhu Houzhao, Emperor Wuzong of Ming, built a Leopard House as well as left and right wings beside the original Tiger House in 1570, the second year of the Zhengde reign. It was extended five years later at a cost of 240,000 taels of silver. Emperor Wuzong was fond of martial arts and hunting. After the Leopard House was built, he frequently stayed there and often neglected government affairs, avoiding the Forbidden City. To protect the emperor, warriors were assigned to accompany him. This plate was cast at the time of Emperor Wuzong. The emperor eventually died in Leopard House.

127-1

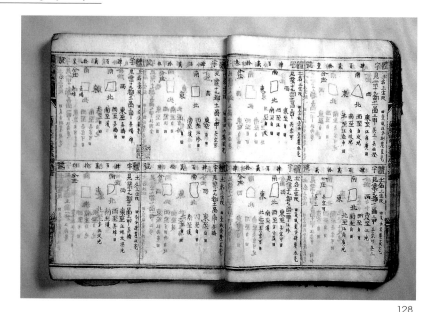

128

128. *Land-Measurement Fish Scale List of the 9th Year of the Wanli Reign* Ming Dynasty. The fish-scale list is the detailed list of land drawn at the time of measuring land throughout the country during the Hongwu reign. It resembled fish-scales, hence the name. There were 56,670,000 hectares of land in China in 1393, the 26th year of the Hongwu reign. At the time of the mid-Ming, bureaucrats, imperial kinsmen and the wealthy took the land of peasants on a large scale and hid their deeds, resulting in the sharp reduction of taxes and other national income. To increase goverement revenue, Zhang Juzheng ordered the nation-wide measurement of land and compiled this illustrated fish-scale list which includes the shape of the 2142 pieces of land, their four boundaries and the owners' names. In that year alone, a total of 9.8 million hectares of concealed land was discovered throughout China.

129. Part of *Picture Scroll on A Survey of Flood Prevention Works* By Pan Jixun; the whole scroll is 45 cm long, 1959 cm wide; colored silk scroll. Pan Jixun (1521-1595), from Wucheng, Zhejiang (present-day Huzhou, Zhejiang Province), served four times as the governor-general of river channels, responsible for 27 years for

129

130

control of the Yellow River, the Huai River and the Grand Canal. During the 276 years of the Ming Dynasty, the Yellow River burst its banks and changed its course 465 times. After the middle Ming, floods were even more frequent, and the Grand Canal was often blocked to transportation. Prime Minister Zhang Juzheng recommended Pan Jixun to be the governor-general of river channels to bring the rivers under control. Pan Jixun summed up his many years of experience in water control as "building embankment to restrain water", "attacking sand with water" and "relieving the canal with the river waters". He wrote *A Survey of Flood-Prevention Works* and sketched this *Picture Scroll on A Survey of Flood-Prevention Works* for the book. In the illustrated scroll, he recorded in writing the years when calamities occurred, the process of bringing them under control and methods for preventing calamities for the hard-to-reach sections on the Yellow River, the Huai River and the Grand Canal, providing full and accurate data for future generations to work in harnessing the rivers.

130. Wei Dazhong's last written words Ming Dynasty.Wei Dazhong (1575-1625), from Jiashan (present-day Jiashan County, Zhejiang Province), passed the imperial examination in the Wanli reign and served as a high official in the judicial department. He was upright and just, and an important member of the Donglin Faction. He insisted on struggle against the eunuch clique and was despised by Wei Zhongxian, the head of that clique. In 1625, the 5th year of the Tianqi reign, eunuch Wei Zhongxian fabricated a complaint claiming unjustly that Wei Dazhong and others had accepted bribes, and he then imprisoned and tortured them. The six officials died tragic deaths in jail. Knowing that it would not be possible to live after arrest, Wei Dazhong inked his last words, saying that he had not been unworthy of his country's trust, but that with great regret, he had ruined his family; he had let down his ancestors and his children.

131. Portrait of San Niangzi Ming Dynasty. San Niangzi (1550-1612), the concubine of Altan Khan of the Tumote tribe of the Mongols, who had won Altan Khan's favor for her intelligence and wisdom. She strongly advocated reconciliation with the Ming court and helped to bring about Altan Khan's title and his paying tribute in 1571, the 5th year of the Longqing reign. The Ming court conferred on Altan Khan the title of "Prince of Loyalty and Obedience," opened up the horse markes in Datong and Zhangjiakou, and promoted trade between the Mongolian

region and inland. When Altan Khan died in 1581, the 9th year of the Wanli reign, San Niangzi controlled the Mongolian people in his stead. The Ming government conferred on San Niangzi the title, "Lady of Loyalty and Obedience", in 1587, the 15th year of the Wanli reign. She ruled the Mongolian people for 32 years, and held to the principle of harmony and friendship between the Mongolians and the people of the Central Plains.

131

End of the Ming Dynasty

In the latter stages of the mid-Ming period, imperial kinsmen and landlords stole the peasants land, as mentioned above. Landless peasants increased day by day, and their burden grew. Along with the constant peasant uprisings and the rise of the Manchus in the northeast, the Ming court, on top of the land tax, levied taxes for suppressing revolts, for warfare in the northeast and for training troops. The peasants suffered unspeakably. In 1627, the 7th year of the Tianqi reign, Wang Er of Chengcheng County, Shaanxi, led the peasants who had resisted the grain levy to storm the county seat and killed the magistrate, the first of several peasants uprisings in the latter years of the Ming Dynasty. The flames of uprising raged in Shaanxi and brought about the great rebellions led by Li Zicheng and Zhang Xianzhong in the last years of the Ming Dynasty. They advanced the slogan "Equality in farm, exemption of farm tax", and thus drew the

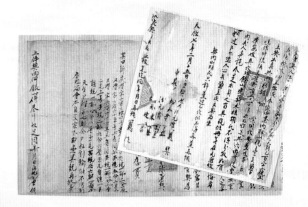

132

alliance of even more peasants. After 18 years of life-and-death struggle, Li Zicheng led the peasant army to invade Beijing in 1644. Emperor Chongzhen hung himself on Coal Hill (present-day Jinshan Hill) and the Ming Dynasty ended this sorry note.

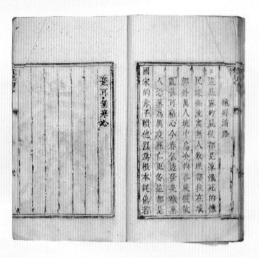

133-1

132. Deed on land sale Ming Dynasty. The purchase and sale of land has occurred since ancient times. Peasants sold farmland, mountain forests and ponds when they were short of money, partularly in time of famine. Peasants who had lost their land became homeless and wandered hither and yon, fomenting major political crises. During the Ming Dynasty, the problem of refugees baffled the Ming government. In the last years of the Ming, many peasants lost their livelihood and were forced to sell their land. In buying and selling land, the general practice was for the seller to find a middleman who would then look for a buyer. The three parties would meet to try to agree on the price and would write a deed which included such details as the name of owner, the reason for selling the land, the serial number of the land, its area, boundaries, agreed price, form of payment and the purchaser's name. The three parties would sign the deed into effect. These two deeds for land sale, carrying the official seal of the government, were legal land transaction deeds.

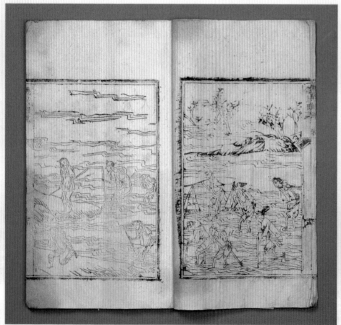

133-2

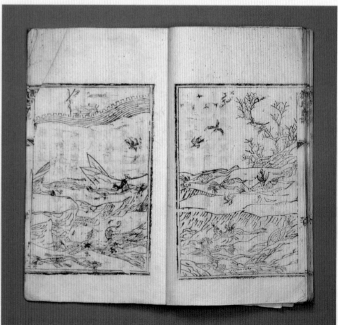

133-3

133. *Illustrated Manual of Famine Refugees*

Illustrations by Yang Dongming. In the later part of the mid-Ming, the Yellow River frequently overflowed its banks, causing great loss of life and property to those living in the middle and lower reaches of the river. In 1593, the 21st year of the Wanli reign, serious flooding occurred in the section of the Yellow River in Henan, and large stretches of farmland and houses were destroyed by the rush of waters, leaving many tragically destitute and homeless. At that time, Yang Dongming, a high supervisory official, personally experienced the disaster. He depicted the flood and the miserable condition among the people after the calamity with drawings and compiled them into a volume, under the title of *Illustrated Manual of Famine Refugees,* to be presented to Emperor Wanli together with his

134-2

memorial to the throne. The illustrated manual was in two parts, drawings and corresponding narrative.

134. Rubbing from tablet recording famine year

Ming Dynasty rubbing 155 cm long, 69 cm wide; discovered in Neihuang County, Henan Province, in 1957. The tablet recorded the miserable sight of natural and man-made disasters and the impoverished life of the Henan region people in the latter years of the Ming Dynasty. This region was hit by disasters every year between 1639 and 1644, the 12th to 17th years of the Chongzhen reign, resulting in very poor harvests, and a skyrocketing price for grain. People were forced to eat bark and wild herbs; barren lands extended across the vast Central Plains; pestilence raged in these areas with most of the people dying, and some even resorted to cannibalism. The description also recorded the activities of Li Zicheng in Henan.

134-1

135-1

136-1

135-2

136-2

135. Copper seal of "Garrison Plantation Department under the Government of Public Works " Full height 8.9 cm, width of each side of the seal-face 7.9 cm, unearthed in May 1959 on Wangfujing Street, Beijing. This was a seal cast by the Dashun regime of Li Zicheng. On the seal-face is carved "Garrison Plantation Department under the Government of Public Works" in seal character. On the

left side of the seal back are carved in regular script in intaglio the characters meaning " □ day of the fourth month of the first year of the Yongchang reign"; on the right side are carved an inscription which reads in translation "Garrison Plantation Department under the Government of Public Works". In 1644, Li Zicheng founded the Dashun regime in Xi'an and called his reign "Yongchang." He

captured Beijing in March that year and ordered that seals be divided into four categories: tally, certificate, deed and stamp. Li Zicheng also changed the six boards (ministries) into "government offices". This copper seal was the evidence of the governmental function of garrison plantation affairs.

136. Copper seal of " Valiant Right Battalion Commander" Ming Dynasty; full height 8 cm, seal-face length 10.6 cm, width 7.1 cm. This was the copper seal cast and issued in Chengdu by the Daxi regime of Zhang Xianzhong. On the seal-face are carved the seal-style characters meaning "Seal of Valiant Right Battalion Commander"; on the right side of the back of the seal are carved in intaglio the name of the seal in regular script; on the left side are carved characters in regular script meaning "Made by the Board of Rites on □ day in the 5th month of the second year of Dashun reign". According to records, the army of the Daxi regime was composed of 102 battalions, all bearing names with political or military significance. Every battalion had a commander, and its seal numbered.

137. Circular on the activities of Li Zicheng issued by the Board of War of the Ming Dynasty Ming Dynasty; 33 cm long, 157.5 cm wide. This circular was issued by the Ming Dynasty Board of War to subordinate entities in various places in 1644, the 17th year of the Chongzhen reign. In the circular, the Ming government reluctantly admitted that the troops of Li Zicheng were accorded an ecstatic welcome by the peasants, and many local officials "opened the city to extend their welcome". The circular demanded that local authorities quickly report any cases of "welcoming the

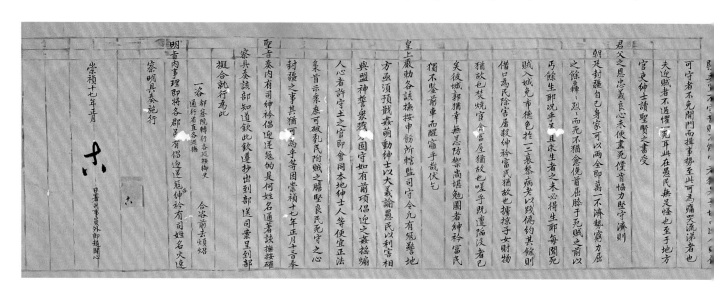

rebels". Two months later, Li Zicheng led his troops to storm and capture Beijing and the Ming Dynasty ended.

138. *Dashun tongbao, yongchang tongbao,* two types of coins *Dashun tongbao* 2.6-2.8 cm in diameter; *yongchang tongbao* 2.5-3.8 cm in diameter. In 1644, the 17th year of the Chongzhen reign, Zhang Xianzhong proclaimed himself emperor, founded the "Daxi" regime, changed his reign title to "Dashun" , set up government entities as well as a mint for coining *dashun tongbao,* currency to be circulated. On the back of the coin were carved the characters "hu"

or "gong", and the value of the coins were "one *jiao* (dime) ", "two *jiao*" and "three *jiao*". In that same year, Li Zicheng proclaimed himself emperor in Xi'an, founded the "Dashun" regime, called his reign "Yongchang", and changed the six boards into " government offices". A mint was set up for coins called *yongchang tongbao.* The large coin was worth one tael of silver; smaller coins were worth five or ten ordinary coins. This was a move to stabilize

139

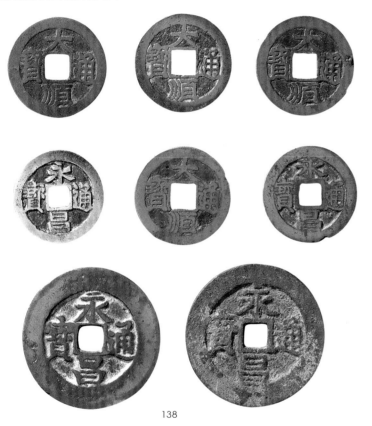

138

prices. It was the usual practice in China, that as a new dynasty came into being, it would create a new currency to confirm its status.

139. Rubbing from tablet on prohibitions issued by a commander of Daxi regime

Ming Dynasty; 129 cm long, 73 cm wide. This was a public notice tablet issued to troops and officials on prohibitions issued by the Daxi regime of Zhang Xianzhong. On the top of the tablet are horizontally carved characters reading in translation "Prohibitions issued by Daxi Cavalry Battalion Commander Liu". According to historical records, the commander of Cavalry Battalion was Liu Jinzhong. On the public notice tablet were listed these prohibitions for officials and soldiers: against raising troops without authorization, against causing trouble in localities, against using coolies and horses at post stations, (for military officers) against accepting lawsuits without authorization, against allowing unsavory elements to join the army, and against marrying local women. The raising of the tablet on prohibitions indicated that the Daxi regime was legally sophisticated.

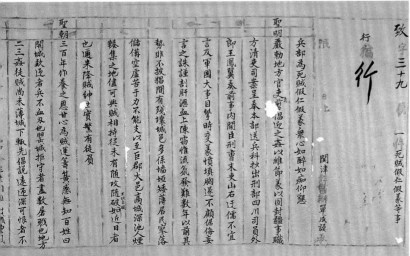

137

Qing Dynasty

(1644–1911)

The Qing Dynasty was the final feudal dynasty in China. The Qing Dynasty reformed the central and local ruling organs and furthered the autocratic centralization of authority. During the Kangxi, Yongzheng and Qianlong periods, complete restoration and overall development took place in agricultural production, and the time was characterized by ecomomic prosperity, social stability, solid national strength and cultural progress. In the vast territory of the country, the unity among the nationalities in China increased. After the reign of Qianlong, however, conflict inside the country and with some foreign countries intensified, and frequent struggles were undertaken against the Qing court. In 1840, the 20th year of the Daoguang reign, the Opium War broke out, in which European capitalists launched an armed invasion into China, the Qing government was forced to conclude a series of treaties under duress, and from that time on China was reduced little by little to the status of semi-colonial, semi-feudal society. Afterwards, class and national conflicts became more and more acute and the

government grew increasingly more corrupt and incompetent. Following an arduous anti-imperialistic, anti-feudal struggle, it was not until the Revolution of 1911, in the third year of the Xuantong reign, that the Chinese people cast out the Qing imperial dynasty which had ruled China for 286 years.

National Unification

After the overthrow of the Ming Dynasty, the Qing troops captured Beijing and set up a system for ruling the whole of China. Most of its ruling policies followed those of the Ming Dynasty, but there were also changes. Its main feature was the establishment of ruling entities with Manchu nobility at the forefront. Decisions on important affairs of national defense and administration were made by the Conference of Princes Regent, whose power surpassed the cabinet and the six boards. During the period of Kangxi, Yongzheng and Qianlong, the Qing government annihilated the separatist forces of Wu Sangui and others, united with Taiwan, suppressed the rebellion of the Junggar tribe, tightened frontier control and established the scope of its vast territory.

The Rise of the Manchus

The Manchus were the descendants of the Nuzhen, which in the early Ming separated into three branches, Maixi, Yeren and Jianzhou Nuzhen. Nurhachi waged a war to unite the three branches of the Nuzhen, and founded the Eight Banner system which combined military affairs and administration during wartime. He founded the "Great Jin" regime in Hetu'ala (present-day Xinbin Manzu Autonomous County, Liaoning Province) in 1616, the 44th year of the Wanli reign of Ming. The regime was called the Later Jin by historians and relocated to Shenyang. After the death of Nurhachi, his son Huangtaiji succeeded him to the throne, changed "Great Jin" to "Great Qing" and renamed Nuzhen as "Manchu". After the death of Huangtaiji, his son Fulin ascended the throne, changed the reign title into "Shunzhi" and appointed Dorgon, the younger brother of Huangtaiji, as regent. After the overthrow of the Ming, Wu Sangui, a Ming general, allowed Qing troops to enter the Shanhai Pass and advanced southward to suppress peasant uprisings together. In May 1644, the Qing troops entered the Shanhai Pass; the Qing regime relocated to Beijing and formally founded the final feudal dynasty to rule the whole of China.

140

140. Portrait of Nurhachi Qing Dynasty. Nurhachi (1559-1626), from Hetu'ala city (present-day Xinbin Manzu Autonomous County, Liaoning Province), a Manchu. He first served under Li Chengliang, a Ming commander, and later raised troops to unite the various branches of the Nuzhen. In 1616, the 44th year of the Wanli reign of Ming, he founded the Later Jin regime.

141. *Tianming tongbao* coins inscribed in Chinese Qing Dynasty; currency; 2.8 cm in diameter; one of the early currencies of the Qing Dynasty, also known as *"tianming hanqian"*. After founding the Later Jin regime in 1616, the first year of the Tianming reign, Nurhachi began to mint *tianming tongbao* using red

copper, and using both the Manchu and Chinese languages, to be circulated in the area ruled by the Later Jin. Its use was abolished after Huangtaiji ascended the throne, and to replace it, the *tiancong tongbao* was minted.

142. *Tiancong tongbao* coins inscribed in the Manchu language Qing Dynasty; currency; 4.9 cm in diameter; one of the early currencies of the Qing Dynasty. In 1626, the 11th year of the Tianming reign of the Later Jin, Huangtaiji ascended the throne, changed his reign title to Tiancong and ordered new coins minted, called *"tiancong tongbao"*. The coin was minted using red copper, bearing both Manchu and Chinese languages and after the Qing

made Beijing its capital, only one coin remained, bearing both Manchu and Chinese languages. The tiancong tongbao ceased to be in circulation after the death of Huangtaiji.

141

142

Founding of the Qing Dynasty

After Shunzhi founded the Qing regime over the entire country, the organizations set up by the central authorities mostly followed the system of the Ming Dynasty, such as the cabinet, the six boards, Court of Censors, and the judiciary. The posts were served by both Manchu and Han officials, but the actual power was in the hands of Manchu officials. The overall military and political power was under the Conference of Princes Regent, and local power was in the hands of civil and military governors, frontier generals and ministers. The civil and military governors, and the generals in border areas took orders directly from the emperor. Qing troops were mainly on the Eight Banner army. The Eight Banner soldiers held their posts through heredity, replaced in old age by Eight Banner youngsters above 16 years of age. Moreover, the Qing government also summoned a large number of Ming troops, armed forces of landlords to surrender and set up the "green battalions".

143-1

143-2

143. The jade seal "Treasure of Emperor" Qing Dynasty; each side of seal-face 16.1 cm in length, heigth of knob 9.8 cm, full height of seal 16.1 cm. It was the practice during the Qing to call the seal of the emperor the "treasure" and the official seal of the emperor the "imperial treasure." In the early Qing, the imperial treasure was housed in the Jiaotai Hall of the Forbidden City, and a department was set up in charge of the seal. In 1746, the 11th year of the Qianlong reign, a total of 25 jade seals were housed in Jiaotai Hall. On this jade seal, with its coiled-dragon-shaped knob, are carved Manchu and Chinese seal-style characters.

144. Seals of *zuoling* of various banners Qing Dynasty; seal height 9.2-9.4 cm, length of the side of seal-face 5.2-5.7 cm. The seals of Manchu military and social entities in the Qing Dynasty were all made of copper, while the style of writing and the seal size varied according to rank of the user. In 1601, the 29th year of the Wanli reign of Ming, Nurhachi set up four banners: yellow, white, red and blue. In 1615, the 43rd year of the Wanli reign, four more banners were begun: xianghuang (yellow-bordered) banner, xiangbai (white-bordered) banner, xianghong (red-bordered) banner and xianglan (blue-bordered) banner. The banners combined as the eight banners, the eight Manchu

banners. There were also eight Mongolian banners and eight Han (Chinese) banners. After the Qing troops entered the Shanhai Pass and following the conviction of Dorgon, the cardinal white banner was recalled by the emperor and put under his direct control. The yellow-bordered banner, cardinal yellow banner and cardinal white banner were made the three upper banners, and the remaining five became the lower banners, to show differences with respect to census register, the civil service system and the military service system, and to carry out a three-level administrative system.The ranks of Manchus, Mongolians, Han troops and slaves were distinctly divided and false claims of rank were forbidden. These seals belonged to *zuoling*, the grass root unit of the eight Han banner troops. *Zuoling* was a rank-four official administering 300 people, and could be either hereditary or nonhereditary.

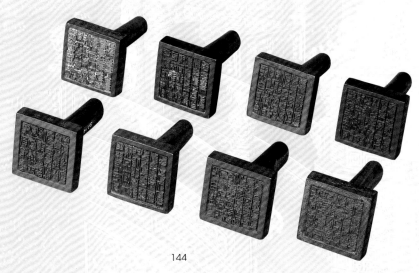

144

145

146

145. Seal of assistant general of the capital police battalion Qing Dynasty; seal-face 10.8 cm high, 6 cm wide. This was the seal of the garrison forces of the Qing capital. The police battalion was a "green battalion" under infantry command. There was a total of five battalions, including cavalry and soldiers for combat and defense, totalling 11,080 men, all under the command of a deputy general. Their mission included defense, patrol and ensuring the security of the capital. An assistant general commanded each of the five battalions; he was under the deputy general, and was in charge of battalion affairs or assisted the general.

146. Seal of city garrison commander of Cangzhou Qing Dynasty; length of each side of seal-facs 8.5 cm, full height 12.4 cm, length of handle 10.1 cm. This was the seal of a city garrison commander of the eight banners in the Qing Dynasty. The city garrison commander was an officer of third rank, controlling the banner register and defense. His position was the same as that of deputy military governor. A city garrison commander was assigned to a city where no general or deputy military governor was assigned. A city garrison commander had under him several hundred to more than 1,000 soldiers. A total of 16 city garrison commanders were assigned throughout the country, among which some were independant garrisons, namely those at Baoding, Cangzhou, Taiyuan and Kaifeng. The city garrison commander had under his command a number of junior officers. He was under the jurisdiction of a general or deputy military governor in a province; in provinces where no such high-ranking officers were stationed, the city garrison

commander came under the control of a provincial military governor. The city garrison commanders of Baoding and Cangzhou, however, were subordinate to the garrison governor stationed in Baodi.

147. Picture showing Duoduo entering Nanjing Qing Dynasty; length 142.1 cm, width 112 cm. Duoduo (1614-1649) was the 15th son of Nurhachi. He received the title of prince in 1620, the 5th year of the

Tianming reign, and was made the master of cardinal white banner in 1626, the 11th year of the Tianming reign. In 1628, the 2nd year of the Tiancong reign, he rendered meritorious service in the expedition against Mongolia by following Huangtaiji, and received the title of "E'erkechuhu'er". Before long he was made *heshuo* Prince Yu. In 1644, the first year of Shunzhi reign, he followed Dorgon into the Shanhai Pass and defeated the rebel peasant army of Li Zicheng; then led troops southward to capture Nanjing and Yangzhou and seized Prince Fu of the Southern Ming. He rode across the battlefield south of the Yangtze River and scored brilliant military achievements. In 1647, the 4th year of the Shunzhi reign, he was promoted to the rank of *fuzheng shude* Prince Yu (a senior prince). He died in 1649, the 6th year of the Shunzhi reign. This picture depicts Duoduo leading the troops into Nanjing.

147-1

148. Portrait of Kangxi Kangxi, namely Aisin-gioro Xuan Ye (1645-1722), a Manchu, ascending the throne at eight years of age, with a reign title of Kangxi. He personally took over the reins of government in 1669, the 8th year of his reign. He put down one after another the revolts of the three feudatories, suppressed the Junggar revolt, united with Taiwan, pacified Tibet and signed the Treaty of Nerchinsk with Russia. He turned his attention to river projects and transport of grain by water to the capital, inspected the south six times, oversaw river projects and came into contact with the upper echelon of Han society. He established the practice of hunting in autumn to win the support of such ethnic minorities as the Mongolians, adopted a policy of "no new taxation for newborn people", and promoted industrial and agricultural production. He respected Neo-Confucianism, compiled the *Collection of Books of Ancient and Modern Times,* but he also frequently launched literary inquisitions to strengthen ideological control. He valued natural science and appointed a Belgian missionary to establish a calendar. He died in 1722 of illness. It was the 61th year of his reign. This portrait was originally housed in the ancestral temple of the Qing imperial family in the Forbidden City.

149. Yellow register of population increase in Wucheng County, Zhejiang Qing Dynasty; 32 cm long, 34 cm wide. This is the population register of Wucheng County, Zhejaing. In 1713, the

148

52nd year of the Kangxi reign, Qing emperor Kangxi issued an order not to ever increase taxes for anyone born in the flourishing age, taking as the standard the number of people in the landtax register of the 50th year of his own reign. Tax would not be increased for anyone born

after that time. These would be called "population newly increased in flourishing age," and a new register would be established. The yellow register was originally the tax and corvée document submitted in the Ming Dynasty. As its cover was yellow, it was called the "yellow register" and was followed in the Qing Dynasty.

150. Imperial robe of Emperor Kangxi Qing Dynasty; length 146 cm, sleeve length 101 cm. This court dress once worn by Emperor Kangxi was made of azurite blue gauze, embroidered with flake gold, with a design of a coiled dragon on the chest, back and sleeves and a design of dragons and the sea between the waist and lower hem, the hem being decorated with flake gold, executed in designs of clouds, dragons and the eight treasures. The attire of the Qing emperor was divided into two major kinds, ceremonial robes and informal dress, and the court costume was one of the main ceremonial robes. The court dress of the Qing emperor preserved the cape and horseshoe-shaped cuff of the Manchu style and the traditional jacket and skirt.

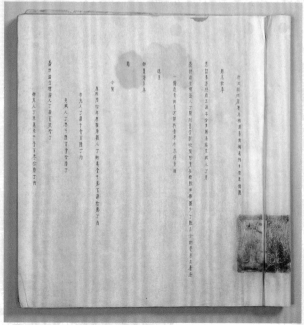

149

151-2

151. Part of an illustrated scroll recording meritorious service   Qing Dynasty; painted by Huang Bi; entire scroll, 714.1 cm long, 40.8 cm wide. Huang Bi, from Yihuang, skilled landscape and figure painter, was especially well-versed in portraiture. This scroll was done in 1677, the 16th year of the Kangxi reign, and depicted the history of the suppression of the revolt of three feudatories by Dong Weiguo. In 1674, the 13th year of the Kangxi reign, Wu Sangui launched a revolt in Kunming, echoed by Geng Jingzhong in Fujian and Shan Zhixin in Guangdong. This was called by historians the "revolt of the three feudatories". As Jiangxi was strategically located between Hubei, Hunan and Guangdong, Wu Sangui closed in on Yuanzhou and Ji'an and Geng Jingzhong attacked Ningdu, Guangchang and Nanfeng. Dong Weiguo, governor-general of Jiangxi, quashed the revolt by both force and pacification, and Jiangxi was subdued. Dong Weiguo then led his troops to Hubei, Hunan and Guizhou, recovering Zhenyuan and staying in Guiyang until the suppression of Yunnan before returning to his post in Jiangxi. On this silk scroll are pictured scenes of the beginning of Dong Weiguo's expedition, his advance on land and water and his return to his post in Jiangxi. The illustrations clearly depict the historical dress, battle array, formation of the honor guard and the variety of weapons.

152. Part of an illustrated scroll of Cai Yurong's southern expedition Qing Dynasty; entire scroll 1102.6 cm long, 52.7 cm wide. This is an illustrated scroll on the suppression of the revolt of Wu Sangui. Cai Yurong (?-1699), courtesy name Ren'an, belonged to the cardinal white banner of Han troops, and served as the governor-general of Hunan-Guangdong. In 1673, the 12th year of the Kangxi reign, Wu Sangui staged a rebellion and war swept across Yunnan, Guizhou, Sichuan and Hunan. Emperor Kangxi dispatched troops to put down the revolt, appointing Cai Yurong, the governor-general of Hubei, Hunan and Guangdong, to defend Jingzhou (present-day Jingzhou City, Hubei Province). He then led naval troops sailing in formidable array into the Dongting Lake where they waged over a dozen fierce battles with Wu Sangui. After the Dongting Lake battles, the Qing troops advanced in four columns to attack both in the front and from the rear. The troops of Wu Sangui retreated in defeat to Zhengyuan, and Cai Yurong continued his victorious pursuit until the pacification of Yunnan. The illustrated scroll of Cai Yurong's southern expedition depicts the scenes of defending Jingzhou, fighting in the Dongting Lake as well as the pacification of Yunnan.

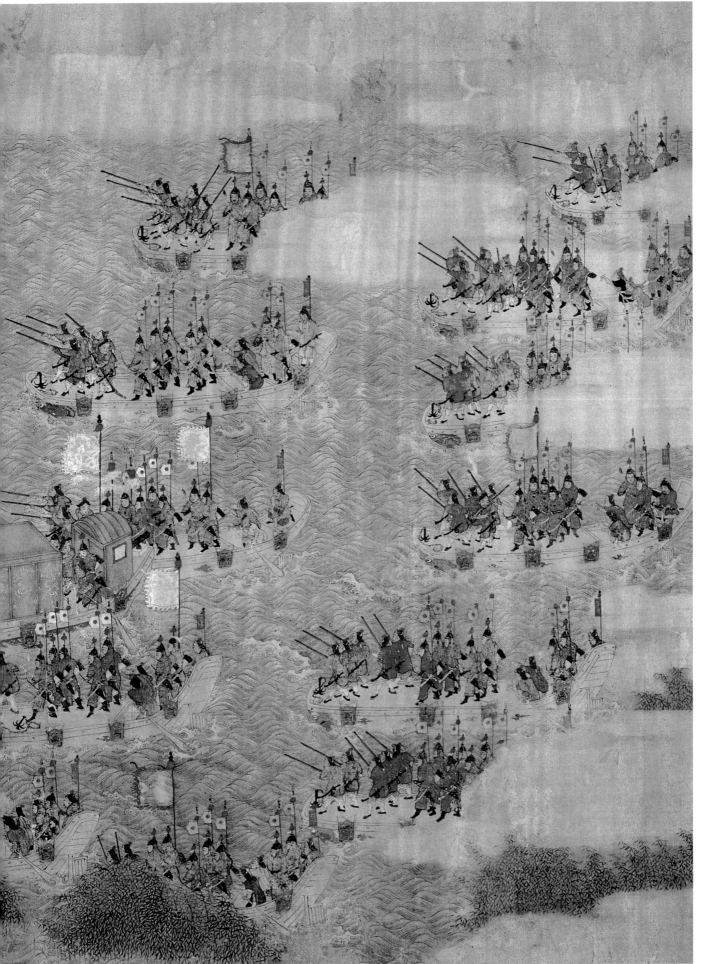

153

153. The portrait of Qianlong

Qianlong, namely Aisin-gioro Hong Li (1711-1799), styled himself Changchun *jushi* (lay Buddhist), as well as "Seventy-year-old Son of Heaven" and, in his old age," Perfect Old Man". He ascended the throne in 1735, the 13th year of the Yongzheng reign, with the reign title of Qianlong. After ascending the throne, he continued to quell the Junggar revolt, suppressed the Big and Small Khwaja incidents and established administrative organs and stationed troops in Xinjiang. He strengthened the administration over Tibet, promulgated the *Constitution on Tibet, By Imperial Order,* and the system of selecting the successors of the Living Buddha, and stationed a minister in Tibet. He installed native officers in areas where national minorities concentrated in the southwest; imposed trade restrictions on Western colonial forces, reduced contact with them and closed some trade ports. He stopped trade at Kyakhta to check the illegal activities of the tsarist Russia. In his old age, he relied heavily on He Shen, as a result of which the administration of officials became corrupt, important legal cases recurred, the White Lotus Society uprising broke out, and from henceforth the Qing Dynasty declined markedly. This portrait was originally housed in the ancestral temple of the Qing imperial family in the Forbidden City.

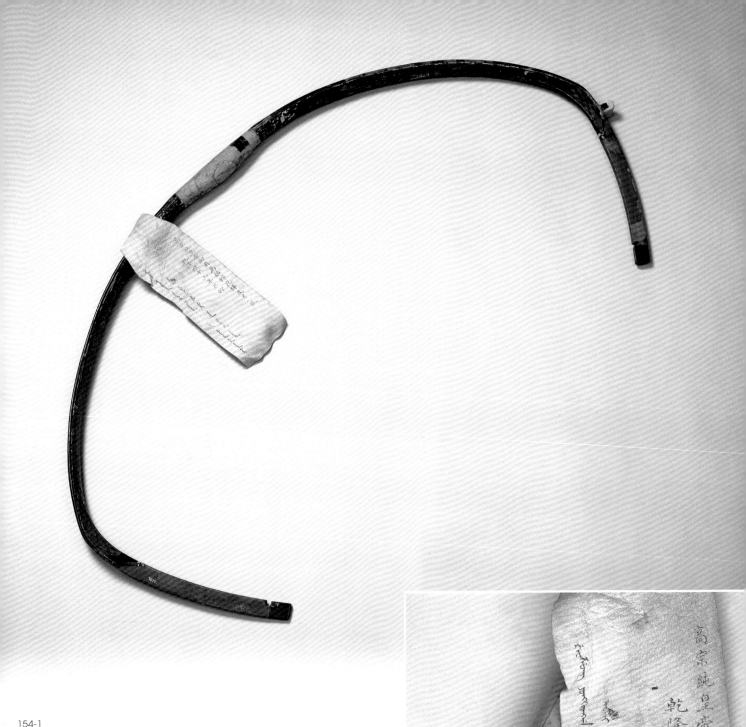

154-1

154. Birch Bow Qing Dynasty; length 170.1 cm, the widest part 4 cm. This bow was used by Qianlong. In the Qing Dynasty, all men, from the emperor down to ordinary soldiers learned martial arts, and carried out military drills regularly every year. Cadets and "green battalion" soldiers also took part in military examinations, and those who were successful in provincial and national military examinations would be awarded corresponding military ranks. In his martial arts practice, the emperor also often used bow and arrow and sword and spear.

高宗純皇帝御用萬福錦花樺皮弓一張

乾隆四十三年恭貯

154-2

155-2

**155. Armor and helmet of Emperor
Qianlong**   Qing Dynasty; height of armor
130 cm, height of helmet 63 cm. This suit
of armor is of brocade, and embellished
all over with gilded copper nails. On the
cape and cuffs are sewn gilded hollow
pieces of mail with sea, cloud and dragon
designs. The armor is in ten parts: gorget,
shoulder pieces, pallette, breastplate,
tuille, front and rear covers and left and
right waistpieces. The armor is also
divided into upper and lower parts, the
coat of mail and the apron. On the coat of
mail are shoulderpieces, armpit-pieces, a
breastplate, a backplate, left and right
covers and waistpieces and a belly
protector under the breastplate. The
helmet is made of black patent leather,
gilded with a hollowed-out design of
cloud, water and dragon and inlaid with
precious stones. On the top are tassels of
sable hair and a big pearl. This suit of
armor was worn by Emperor Qianlong
when hunting or reviewing troops.

155-1

Further Consolidation of Unified, Multinational China

During the Qing Dynasty, the political, economic and cultural relations among various nationalities became increasingly harmonious, reinforceing the foundation of national unity. In the earlier Qing period, the Chinese nation repeatedly struggled against foreign aggression and to safeguard national unity. In this protracted struggle, the people of various nationalities developed and defended the national frontier of China and contributed to the further consolidation and development of a unified, multinational country.

156

156. Portrait of Zheng Chenggong   Qing Dynasty; painted by Huang Zi; 130.5 cm long, 65 cm wide. Zheng Chenggong (1624-1662), original name Sen, courtesy name Damu, from Nan'an, Fujian. In 1661, he led troops to Taiwan and drove out the Dutch colonialists. After recovering Taiwan, Zheng Chenggong set up Chengtian and Anping prefectures, and Tianxing and Wannian counties; he encouraged the reclamation of wasteland by army units and people, developed manufacturing and established schools. He was greatly admired. In the portrait, Zheng Chenggong wears a square kerchief and a full suit of armor, and he is playing chess with someone. On the lower right of the picture a petty officer who has just dismounted is kneeling and reporting the current military situation. On the left of the picture is the name of the painter together with his seal in intaglio.

157. *Veritable Records of Expedition*   Qing Dynasty; written by Yang Ying. This book records the events relating to the recovery of Taiwan by Zheng Chenggong. Yang Ying was from Fujian, and the exact date of his birth and death are unknown. He was an official under Zheng Chenggong, whom he followed for a long time, and was in charge of financial and administrative affairs. After the death of Zheng Chenggong, he continued to hold a post in Zheng's regime for some 30 years. He was responsible mainly for the secretariat, raising of funds and provisions as well as accounting. He was also very familiar with the military and political affairs of Zheng Chenggong and so he was able to write this account. The records start and end, not with the life of Zheng Chenggong, but with Yang Ying's participation. Though Yang was not an educated man, and the historical material he recorded is very simple and unadorned, yet the events he recorded here are complete and well-documented. The book preserves much original and first-hand information such as orders, which are very important data for studying Zheng Chenggong.

157

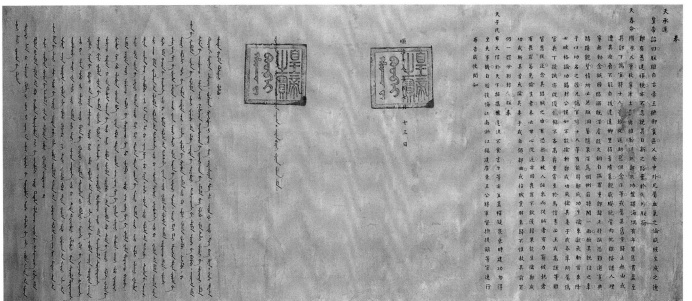

158

159

158. Edict to offer amnesty to troops under Zheng Chenggong Qing Dynasty; 183 cm long, 78 cm wide.The first part of the edict was written in Chinese characters in regular script, followed by the inscription "the 13th day of the leap month of the 18th year of the Shunzhi reign" and affixed with the seal of the "Treasure of the Emperor". In August 1659, the 16th year of the Shunzhi reign, Zheng Chenggong and Zhang Huangyan jointed forces to advance northward to the Yangtze River, captured Guazhou and Zhenjiang, and besieged Jiangning (present-day Nanjing, Jiangsu Province). The imperial court was shocked by their momentum. However, his underestimation of the enemy led to his defeat. Zheng Chenggong retreated to Xiamen with his troops and was ready to attack Taiwan. It was then that the Qing government issued this edict summoning troops of Zheng Chenggong to surrender.

159. Military "national surname bottle" Qing Dynasty; ammunition; height 19.7 cm, calibre 16 cm, bottom diameter 5.3 cm. This was the type of bomb used by Zheng Chenggong's troops. Zheng Chenggong received the surname Zhu, that of the imperial family, in the Longwu reign of the Southern Ming period and was made Count of Loyalty and Filial Piety, so he was addressed respectfully as the "lord of national surname", and this kind of bottle bomb was called "national surname bottle". The "national surname bottle" spread widely in southern Fujian. Many were found in Shijing Village in Nan'an, Guiyu in Jinjiang and Hanjiang, mostly found in the sea by fishermen, but some were unearthed on land. They were very much the same, made of pottery with small mouth, deep belly, and small flat bottom. As they rested on the seafloor for a long time, their surfaces are covered with barnacles. Such bottles were filled with gun powder and iron sand.Their explosive force after ignition was very powerful. These devices were used in large numbers in battles against Dutch colonialists and to recover Taiwan.

**160. Part of illustrated scroll of inspection
tour in Taiwan**   Qing Dynasty; entire scroll
137.5 cm long, 55.5 cm wide. In 1683, the
Qing government sent troops across the sea;
Zheng Keshuang, the grandson of Zheng
Chenggong, surrendered, and the Qing court
united with Taiwan. In 1722, the 61st year of
the Kangxi reign, the Qing government set up
the post of Censor for Taiwan. This picture
depicts the Censor for Taiwan inspecting
Taiwan during the Yongzheng reign. One
Manchu and one Han censor were sent each
year by the Court of Censors to inspect
Taiwan, where they resided in the prefectural
city during their one-year term of office.
Those achieving good results would remain
in office for a second year. Later the term of
office was increased to three years. The
duties of the Censor for Taiwan were 1)
supervision over the officials at all levels in
Taiwan concerning their performance in
government administration; 2) submission of
impeachment proceedings to the central
authorities from time to time to prevent the
unlawful practices of local officials; 3) the
review and adjudiction of outstanding cases;
4) recommendations on the establishment of
local entities; 5) recommendations for the
promotion and demotion of officials and
officers; 6) supervision of and encouraging
local officials to suppress disturbances and
stabilize the local situation; and 7) urging
local troops to strictly carry out sea defense
as well as to concern themselves with
economic, cultural and educational
undertakings.

The appointment of the Censor for Taiwan
reinforced relations between the central
authorities of the Qing court and Taiwan and
promoted the social, economic and cultural
development of the Taiwan region. In 1785,
the 50th year of the Qianlong reign, the
appointment of the Censor for Taiwan was
discontinued, and the inspection of Taiwan
fell to the governor-general,the provincial
military governor, the General of Fuzhou,
and the provincial commander-in-chief of
naval forces and of land forces. Either the
governor-general, the provincial military
governor or the two provincial commanders-
in-chief was required to sail across the sea in
rotation to inspect Taiwan and examine in
detail the governmental affairs of Taiwan.

Map showing boundaries set between China and Russia by the Treaty of Nerchinsk

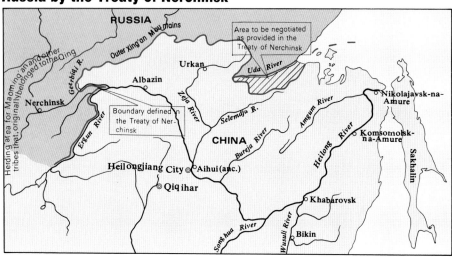

161

and Han (Chinese) languages, and believed in a form of Shamanisn. At the time of Kangxi, when Russia invaded northeast China, the Hezhen people, along with the Qing troops and many other nationalities, actively joined the heroic struggle against the invaders.

163. Portrait of Oroqen   Collected from *Picture of Taxation and Tribute* of the Qing Dynasty; entire scroll 1438 cm long, 33.8 cm wide. The Oroqen people are found in the Greater and Lesser Xing'an Mountains in Heilongjiang Province, China, mainly hunters and farmers. They established private ownership, but retained the remnants of primitive communes, and believed in a form of Shamanism. At the time of Kangxi, when Russia invaded northeast China, the Oroqen people also actively participated in the struggle.

161. Map showing boundaries set between China and Russia by the Treaty of Nerchinsk   The vast area of the Heilong River valley has been Chinese territory since ancient times. In the mid-17th century, tsarist Russia sent troops across the Stanovoj-Chrebet mountains, invading the Heilong River valley; they burned, killed and looted wherever they went, but encountered the heroic resistence of the Qing troops and local people of various nationalities. The tsarist Russian troops set up strongholds in the middle and lower reaches of the Heilong River, forcibly levied tributes and taxes and tried in vain to occupy this land. In 1685, the 24th year of the Kangxi reign, Peng Chun led troops to attack Albazin and defeated the tsarist Russian troops. Both sides withdrew. In the following year, the tsarist Russian troops again invaded Albazin. Sabusu led the Qing troops again to attack and defeat the tsarist Russian troops. In 1689, the 28th year of the Kangxi reign, China and Russia signed the Treaty of Nerchinsk, providing that from the Stanovoj-Chrebet mountains to the sea, the boundaries should be delimited by the Geerbiqi and Ergun rivers, confirming legally that the vast area of the Heilong River and Wusuli River valleys south of the Stanovoj-Chrebet mountains belonged to China.

162. Portrait of Hezhen   Collected from *guang yu sheng lan,* a pictorial album of the Qing Dynasty. The Hezhen people are mainly distributed in Tongjiang, Fuyuan and Raohe counties, having tribal relations with the ancient Heishui Mohe and Yeren

Nuzhen tribes. As they wore fishskins and used dogs, they were also known as the "fishskin tribe" or "dog-using tribe." They lived on fishing, used both the Manchu

162

關東
鄂倫綽

寧古塔之東北海島一帶唐書所云少海之北三面阻海人依興散居有魚鹽之利
者人有數種鄂倫綽其一也在近海之多羅河強黔山遊牧男女皆披髮跣足以養
角鹿捕魚為生所居以魚皮為帳性懦弱歲進貂皮

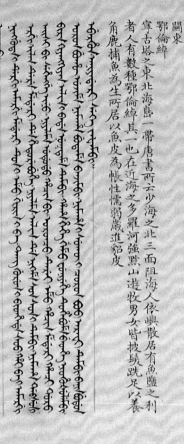

164. *Picture Album on Supervising Grain Transport for Northern Expedition* Qing Dynasty; length 41.1 cm, width 38.4 cm. In 1677, the 16th year of the Kangxi reign, Galdann, chieftain of the Junggar tribe, staged a revolt aimed at splitting the country. Emperor Kangxi dispatched 100,000 soldiers to put down the revolt along three routes—central, western and eastern. The Qing government decreed: "In addition to an 80-day grain ration, every soldier will be entitled to two decalitres of rice to be provided by Hutan Hesu (present-day Hekou of Inner Mongolia Autonomous Region), and all the carts, horses, mules, fodder and the ration of the cart pullers will be provided by the provincial military governor of Shanxi." Grain transport corps composed of 200 carts, more than 200 conscripted laborers and nearly 1,000 mules and horses transported some 200,000 kilograms of

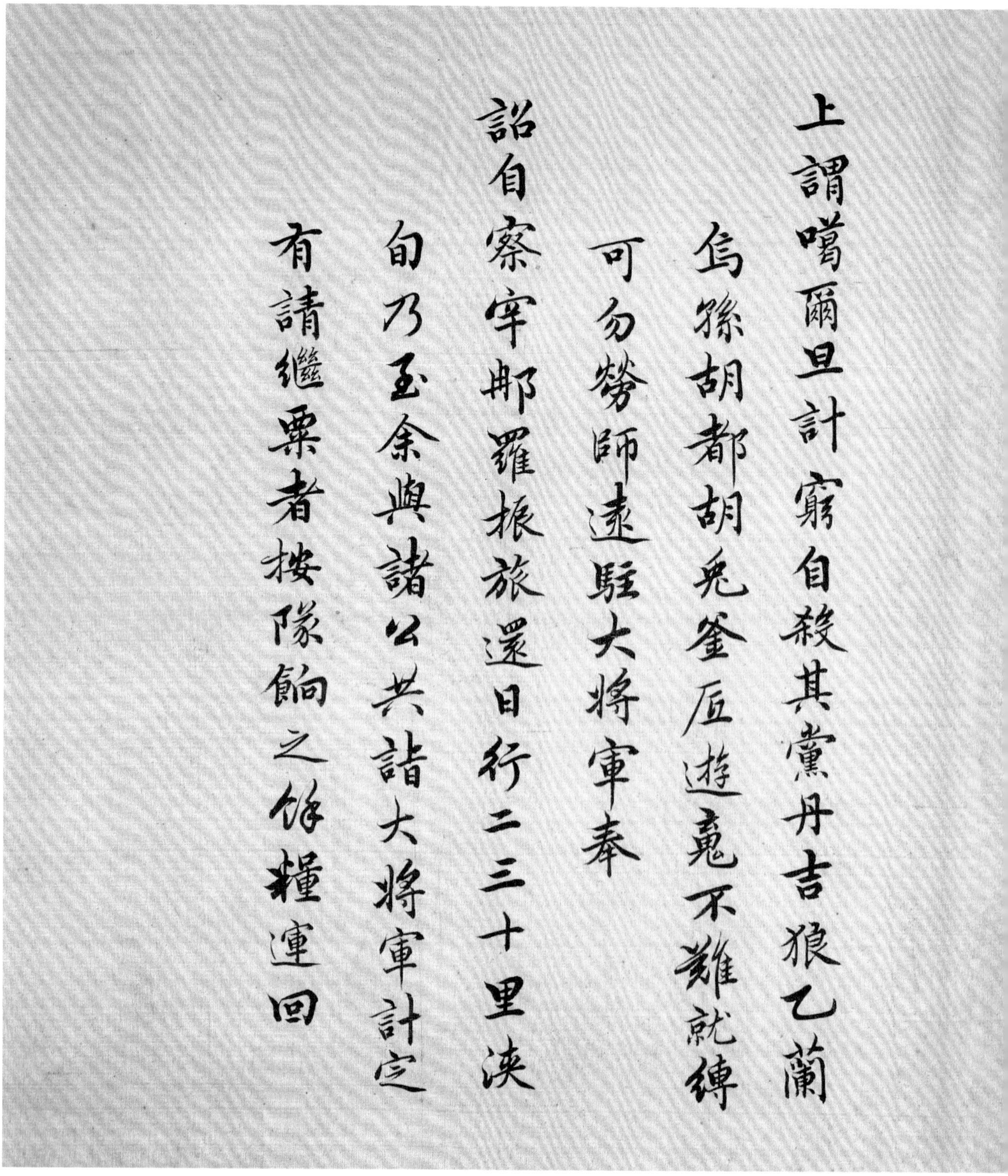

上謂噶爾旦計窮自殺其黨丹吉狼乙蘭

烏孫胡都胡兆釜厄遊寇不難就縛

可勿勞師遠駐大將軍奉

詔自察宰邨羅振旅還日行二三十里淀

旬乃至余與諸公共詣大將軍計定

有請繼粟者按隊餉之餘糧運回

army provisions. There were eight such grain transport corps on the western route, which crossed steep mountains and deep rivers, trudged through the Gobi and other broad deserts, transporting army provisions continuously to the front at Kelulun River. The *Picture Album on Supervising Grain Transport for Northern Expedition* was painted from the experience of Fan Chenglie, the army provision transport supervising officer of the western route army for suppressing the Junggar revolt. Fan Chenglie, courtesy name Yangong, was appointed the army provision transport supervising officer for the western route army in 1695, the 34th year of the Kangxi reign, when he served as royal tutor. The album originally had 48 pages but now only 38 pages remain, and for each page half is a colored illustration in fine brushwork, and the other half, a brief description of the illustration in the hand of Fan Chenglie himself. In the illustrations, the cities, stations, mountains and rivers, the distance of routes, the officers, soldiers and conscripted laborers, carts and horses are all vividiy depicted in detail. It is a priceless illustrated historical documents.

164

165. Part of an illustrated scroll on the western expedition of the "Remote-pacification General" Qing Dynasty; entire scroll 692 cm long, 49 cm wide. This scroll depicts the suppression of Junggar revolt in Tibet by the Qing Dynasty. In 1716, the 55th year of the Kangxi reign, Cewang'alabutan led troops into Tibet, seized and killed Lazang Khan, destroyed monasteries and massacred the people, plunging Tibet into disorder. In 1720, the 59th year of the Kangxi reign, the Qing government "ordered Remote-pacification General Yun Ti to lead troops to enter Tibet" to put down the revolt. The picture shows the troops under Galbi advancing towards Tibet from the south. The beginning of the scroll shows Fala, a Qing military governor, entering and garrisoning in Dajianlu, and Yue Zhongqi, a deputy general, entering and garrisoning in Litang. The illustration vividly shows how the Qing troops, with the support of the Tibetan people and Eleut Mongolian people, united with the Tibetan tribal chief and headman to enter Qamdo (present-day Qamdo County, Tibet Autonomous Region), Zha'yab (present-day Zhag' yab County, Tibet Autonomons Region) and reached Lhorongzong (present-day Lhorong County, Tibet Autonomous Region), where they met rebel resistence. Balbi led the troops to Lali and joined forces with Yue Zhongqi to capture Maizhokunggar on August 5,1720. The illustration shows Galbi and other generals leading troops forward, welcomed by the people of various nationalities who lined the streets. Afterwards, the Qing troops forced their way across the Lhasa River, entering Lhasa the next day in three columns. Several thousand Junggars surrendered. Finally, formations of troops are shown in front of the Potala Palace and on both sides of the Jokhong Monastery. The images shown are "forcing their way across the Lhasa River" and "entering Lhasa."

166. Part of illustrated scroll on suppressing the Junggar rebellion Qing Dynasty; painted by Qian Weicheng; entire scroll 808 cm long, 41 cm wide. This is a historical illustrated scroll depicting the suppression of the Junggar (Dawaqi) revolt in Xinjiang by Qing troops. Dawaqi of the Junggar tribe led troops to occupy Ili and the Qing government, in November 1754, the 19th year of the Qianlong reign, ordered "generals Bandi and Amulsana, on the northern route, and generals Yongchang and Salale, on the western route... to lead their troops to advance forward to suppress the Junggar tribe." The album begins by showing the western route army passing through Hami. When the troops arrived at Barkol, the illustration shows the people of Eleut Mongolian tribes and the Uygur welcome the troops with sheep and wine. Beyond the joining of forces at Boltala (present-day Boluo County, Xinjiang Uygur Autonomous Region), the Ili River appears in the picture. This is basically consistent with historical facts. The surprise attack of Ayuxi on the camp of Dawaqi is the only scene of fighting in the scroll. Ayuxi and two other warriors led 22 cavalrymen into enemy camps in the dead of night, resulting in the routing of nearly 10,000 rebels. More than 7,000 surrendered to the Qing camps. Dawaqi led about 2,000 men escaping into southern Xinjiang, appealing Huojis Boke, Uygur chieftain in Wushi, for shelter. Boke captured him and turned him over to the Qing army command. The illustration shows the Ili River and the scene of surrender at the Qing troop headquarters.

166-1

166-2

167

167. Black flannel bag and quiver with silver ornaments   Qing Dynasty; bow bag and arrow quiver; bow bag 62 cm long, 29 cm wide, quiver 42 cm long, 21 cm wide. This was a gift presented by the Tu'erhute tribe to Emperor Qianlong. Tu' erhute was one of the four sections of the Oyrat Mongolians in the Qing Dynasty, who were originally a nomadic tribe in Yal, near Ta'erbahatai in Xinjiang. At the end of the Ming and in the early Qing, the Tu'erhute tribe moved westward to the lower reaches of the Ejile River (present-day Volga).Later, as the people of the tribe could not bear the oppression of tsarist Russia, they rebelled. The year was 1756, the 21st year of the reign of Qianlong, and they revolted under the leadership of Cuizabu and the son of Ayuqi, the leader of the Tu'erhute tribe. After three years, they returned to China. Emperor Qianlong received them in the imperial resort in Rehe and honored them with banquet at Wanshu Garden at the Chengde Summer Resort. On behalf of Dundashi, Cuizabu presented tribute to Emperor Qianlong, among the gifts these black flannel bags (bow bag and arrow quiver) encrusted with silver ornaments. On the sheepskin stripe on the bow bag and arrow quiver was written "Tu'ergute Taijidunduobu Dashi respectfully presents bow bag and arrow quiver, in the 21 year of the Qianlong reign". As to the return of the Tu'erhute tribe, the Qing government gave them favorable aid and arrangements, assigned a hunting area for them, set up the "zhasake" (appointment of officials) system, and designated senior officials who would come under the jurisdiction of the Ili General.

168. Picture Album of Moslem Area in the Western Regions Qing Dynasty; every half leaf 43.9 cm long, 36.8 cm wide. The Western Regions was the overall name for the entire area to the west of the Yumen Pass in the Western Han Dynasty. The name of Western Regions was abolished at the end of the 19th century. This illustrated album depicts the social life of the ethnic minorities in the north and south of Xinjiang.The term "Eleut" was the overall name for various tribes in western Mongolia in the Qing Dynasty.

The Eleut were divided into four sections: Du'erbote, Junggar, Tu'erhute and Heshuote. They lived in the Zapen River valley and the Junggar Basin, and were engaged in animal husbandry and a little agriculture. The Tu'erhute tribe moved to the lower reaches of the Volga River in search of pasture at the end of Ming and in early Qing. They returned to China at the time of Qianlong and received permission to move around in Ili. The Illustration depicts the nomadic life of the Tu'erhute tribe.

169. Silver statue of the Fifth Dalai Lama
Qing Dynasty; height 50.5 cm. Ngag-dbang blo-bzang rgya-mtsho(1617-1682), the Fifth Dalai Lama, was born in Qonggyai, Shannan, Tibet. In 1652, the 9th year of the Shunzhi reign, the Fifth Dalai Lama led a retinue of 3,000 men to reach Beijing at the invitation of Emperor Shunzhi. He met the emperor at the South Garden and stayed in the Yellow Monastery that had been specially built for him. He left Beijing in February the following year to return to Tibet. When he reached Dege in May, the minister of rites and the deputy minister in charge of national minority affairs dispatched by Emperor Shunzhi also arrived to confer on him the gold writ and gold seal from the emperor, and the emperor also conferred on the Dalai Lama a title of honor. After returning to Tibet, he used the gold and silver granted by Emperor Shunzhi to build 13 monasteries of the Dge-lugs-Pa Sect in Tibet. This silver statue of the Fifth Dalai Lama was presented by him to the emperor when he was in Beijing.

170-1

170. Gold seal of the Fifth Dalai Lama (reproduction) Qing Dynasty; each side of the seal-face 11.3 cm wide, the seal 9.9 cm high. The Dalai Lama is one of the two religious leaders of the Tibetan Buddhism (Yellow Sect),on an equal par with the Panchen Lama. Emperor Shizu of the Qing Dynasty formally conferred on the Fifth Dalai Lama the title "Dalai Lama," and recognized his political and religious position in Tibet. This gold seal was issued by the Qing government to the Fifth Dalai Lama.

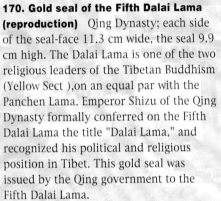

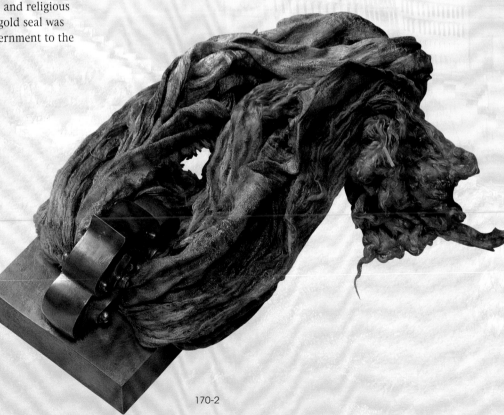

170-2

171. Writ conferring title of Seventh-generation Panchen Erdrni (reproduction) Qing Dynasty; a total of 13 folds, 134 cm long, 22.5 cm wide, 5,750 grams in weight. This is the gold writ issued to the Panchen Lama by the Qing government. In 1713, the 52nd year of the Kangxi reign, the Qing government sent officials to enter Tibet to formally confer on the Fifth Panchen Lama, Lobsang Yeshe, the title of "Panchen Erdeni" and presented him with a gold seal and gold writ. This was the beginning of the title of Panchen Erdeni, and from that time on the religious position of the Panchen was affirmed by the the central government of the Qing Dynasty. In 1728, the 6th year of the Yongzheng reign, the Qing government placed Lhaze, Ngamring and Pıncogling of southern Tibet under the jurisdiction of the Panchen Erdeni.

172. Imperial order conferring on Awangdanjin the title of Teacher of the Nation, Jingjue Monastery Qing Dynasty; 189.5 cm long, 56.7 cm wide. The Jingjue Monastery is located in the present-day Qinghai Province. In this order issued in 1701, the 40th year of the Kangxi reign, Awangdanjin was highly praised for his proficiency in religious discipline and for his open-minded nature, and received the title of Teacher of the Nation of Jingjue Monastery. The Qing Government considered the administration of Tibet to be extremely important and exerted great influence upon the political, economic and cultural development of the Tibetan region.

171

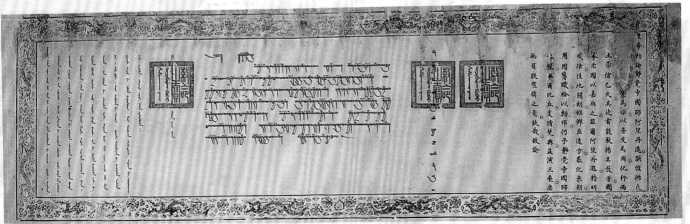

172

Social Life of Various Ethnic Minorities

The minorities in the Qing Dynasty were colorful and varied in their customs—eating, clothing, shelter, transport, marriages and funerals, festivals, culture and recreation, social contact, customs and habits and forms of disaster relief. Because of the vastness of territory and the multitude of nationalities, the national economic and cultural traditions were different and the relations among various ethnic groups were complex and changeable. Therefore, it was necessary for nationalities to exchange and learn from one another, to promote social development and to improve living standards overall.

173. Portion of illustration: wedding in the Qing period   Qing Dynasty; whole scroll 369.5 cm in length, 35 cm in width. In the Qing Dynasty, the wedding of the Han people took the form of bringing the bride to the groom's. In different areas, however, the wedding customs differed. In this illustration scroll, the bride rides a donkey with the groom by her side, followed by a group of well-wishers. It seems to represent the form of weddings in the northern and northwestern part of China. After the arrival of the bride, the wedding banquet and mutual congratulations will follow. In the picture many guests gather together and propose toasts, a scene of bustling excitement.

173-1

174-1

174. Painting showing worship at Mt. Miaofeng Qing Dynasty; 205.5 cm long, 114.6 cm wide. This is a folk painting reflecting the temple fair at Mt. Miaofeng in Beijing. It is a visual history for studying the social life, customs and beliefs in Beijing in the Qing dynasty.Mt. Miaofeng is located in the suburbs northwest of Beijing, some 35 kilometers from the capital. In the Taoist temples of Mt. Miaofeng, Princess Bi Xia, who has been considered loftiest among women, is consecrated. For this reason, most pilgrims to Mt. Miaofeng are women. Temple fairs at Mt. Miaofeng would drew many pilgrims as well as a wide variety of goods offered for sale and diverse folk activities.

175

175. Woman's riding jacket made of blue Zhangzhou satin with colored lace Qing Dynasty; length 61.5 cm. The woman's riding jacket is a short gown with buttons down the front dressed outside the garment. Formerly the jacket was worn by the Manchu people while riding, hence its name. It is shorter than the usual outer gown, usually made in a variety of styles and of nice material. Such jackets were increasingly popular after the Kangxi and Yongzheng period. Zhangzhou satin is a traditional silk fabric of China, produced in Zhangzhou, Fujian Province.

176

176. Lilic woven skirt made of Huzhou silk fabric with colored embroidery

Qing Dynasty; 103 cm in length. Pure raw silk was used as both the warp and weft of the Huzhou silk fabrics, finished after weaving and dyeing. These real silk fabics were produced as early as the Warring States period. The fabric was thin and elastic and the clothing and skirts made of it were pleasantly cool to wear. There was a great variety of skirts in the Qing Dynasty. This lilac-weave skirt made of Huzhou silk features exquisite colored embroidery and was typical of the Qing Dynasty.

177. Part of *Picture Scroll on Taxation and Tribute* Qing Dynasty; painted by Jin Tingbiao and others; entire scroll 1438 cm in length, 33.8 cm in width. Jin Tingbiao, from Wucheng, Zhejiang(present-day Huzhou, Zhejiang Province), a skilled painter, served in the palace. This scroll records the life and taxation and tribute levied on various nationalities during the Qing Dynasty. In 1751, the 16th year of his reign, Emperor Qianlong ordered "the governors-general and military governors along the border to have paintings made to reflect the dress of the Miao, Yao, Li and Zhuang people under their jurisdiction, as well as foreigners, and present them to the Privy Council for transmitting to the Emperor, so as to show the prosperity of the empire." In this way, the provincial

governors and provincial military governors all over the country sent artists to execute these paintings which were then submitted to the Qing governmant for the perusal of the emperor. Later, Jin Tingbiao and others based the *Picture Scroll on Taxation and Tribute* on those paintings. The first part of the scroll covers vassal states and foreign countries and the rest the various nationalities in the country; altogether comprising 300 sets, each set including pictures of men and of women separately, making a total of 600 pictures. Each picture is annotated in both the Manchu and Chinese languages, explaining the history, dwelling place, production, living conditions and taxes and tribute paid to the imperial government.

177-2

177-1

178-1

178. Qianlong *famille-rose* pot   Qing
Dynasty; 45 cm high, 13.6 cm wide at the rim.
This was a porcelain item baked in the
government kiln in 1736-1795 during the
Qianlong period. In the Qing Dynasty, these
pots with peculiar shapes were used specially
in the palace or by the upper classes of
Mongolia and Tibet for drinking milk.

178-2

178-3

179. Kazak embroidered dress Qing Dynasty; 142 cm long. The Kazak people are mainly distributed around Ili and Barkol. They engaged in animal husbandry and their dress reflects the characteristics of the pastoral area, namely using skin and fur for their garments. For riding, the dress is generally loose and wide. Their woolen dresses are brightly colored, adorned with lace and embroidery. The collar of the underwear is usually high, and is turned down to cover the collar of the outer garment. This Kazak embroidered dress is in exquisite, typical style.

180. Uygur floral flannel on green background Qing Dynasty; woolen knitwear; 371 cm in length, 41.3 cm in width. Where the Uygur people live is rich in sheep's wool, and the skill of the local people in making woolen fabrics is time-honored. This piece of floral flannel takes green wool as warp and weft. The fabric is plain with a colored floral flannel woven into it. The Uygur colored unlined long gown made of this kind of floral flannel is exquisite.

181. Tibetan bronze ewer with dragon-shaped handle   Qing Dynasty; container; 33.8 cm high. This ewer would be used by the Tibetan people to hold buttered tea. The Tibetan people, distributed in Tibet, Sichuan and Qinghai, take roasted *qingke* barley flour, beef and mutton as staple foods and drink highland barley wine and buttered tea. Buttered tea is made by stewing brick tea, to which butter and salt are added, then pounding and mixing it in a wooden tub. The more butter, the better the quality of the tea. Buttered tea is a first-rate daily drink among the Tibetan people and is also a common drink served to guests.

181-1

181-2 ▷

182

182. Daur embroidered tobacco bag
Qing Dynasty; everyday item; 20 cm long,
6.5 cm wide. This is a small bag to hold
cut tobacco. The Daur people, living in
Inner Mongolia and Heilongjiang, make a
living from agriculture and hunting. They
do not have their own language; also
believe in a form of Shamanism. The Daur
people, both men and women, smoke, so
small tobacco bags are important to them.
Many tobacco bags are meticulously made
using fine materials, and are often
embroidered with colorful designs.

183. Oroqen embossed birch box Qing
Dynasty; household article; 10.1 cm high.
The Oroqen people are hunters who dwell
in conical structures made of birch poles
covered with birch leaves and leading a
very simple life. As the place abounds
with birches, many household items of the
Oroqen people are made of birch bark,
such as basins, bowls, tubs, chests and
boxes,to hold food and sundry articles.
This embossed birch box is used to hold
small items.

184

184. Coral silver-tassel headgear of Yi people   Qing Dynasty; 130 cm in length. The Yi people mainly live in the Greater and Lesser Liang Mountain, and engaged primarily in agriculture; they have their own Yi language and are polytheists. The dress of the Yi people has its own special features and the headgear of men and women are different. Men use a piece of blue cloth several meters long to wrap their heads, leaving a slender conical part of the cloth protruding in the front. Women usually wrap their heads with a black kerchief, whereas young women wear embroidered square kerchieves with the front part covering the forehead. The wealthy use finely crafted silver headgear in the shape of chain or an ear of grain.

185. Brocade waistband of Yao people

Qing dynasty; ornament, token; 176 cm long, 5.3 cm wide. The Yao people are found in Guangxi and neighboring provinces, and are farmers. They do not have a separate language; they are also polytheists. The dress of the Yao men and women resembles that of the Zhuang people, and both men and women wear waistbands. These are very long, mostly of blue silk which they weave and dye themselves, and on which are woven or embroidered various decorative patterns. For the Yao people, a waistband is also a token of love.

186. Dai sword with ivory hilt and silver sheath

Qing Dynasty; 43.4 cm long. The Dai men wear swords because of the need in work and daily life. While involved in labor, the men all carry iron choppers with a wooden hilt. The choppers are long or short, and are for chopping grass or trees to clear the land. In daily life they carry small iron knives with a wooden hilt; those with higher social status carry meticulously made knives with an ivory or bone hilt and a silver sheath. At festive gathering, country fairs and other occasions, they all wear such knives at the waist. Such small knives are generally used for peeling fruit, cutting food or as a kind of ornament.

187. Zhuang brocade with bird design and yellow background

Qing Dynasty; full length 131.7 cm, width 86.6 cm. The Zhuang people are distributed in Guangxi and neighboring provinces. They were called Liao, Li and Liang in ancient times and Zhuang since the Song Dynasty. The Zhuang people are also farmers and practice a polytheist belief. Zhuang brocade is also known as "velveteen quilt", and is thick and heavy. According to historical records, Zhuang brocade is produced in various prefectures and counties in Guangxi. Garments and skirts of the Zhuang people are all made of colored velvet and woven with cloth in the shape of bird or flower. It looks spectacular from a distance but rough up close. The Zhuang brocade uses the cotton or jute thread as the warp to be woven with twisted or slightly twisted color weft to form symmetrical patterns on the front and back of the fabrics, completely covering the fabric with designs, adding thickness. The Zhuang brocade is brilliantly colored, strong in contrast, even gaudy, and is most suitable for making packsacks, apron, tablecloths and other household items.

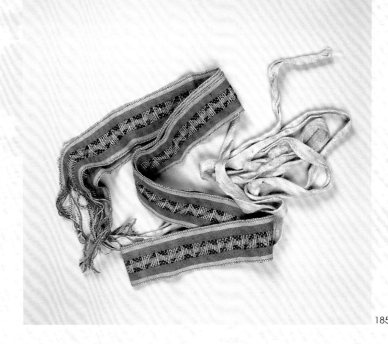

185

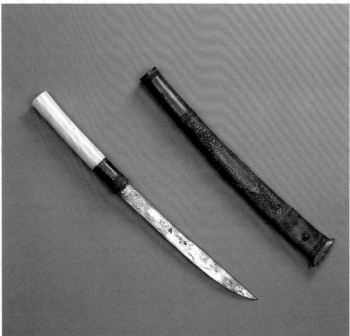

186

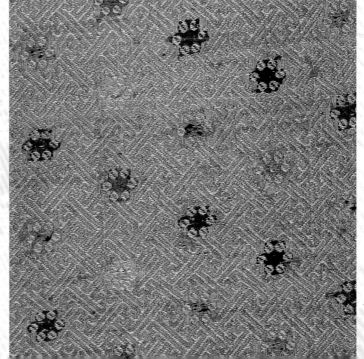

187

番戲

番婦為戲名曰做田衣錦紵簪珠花一老番鳴金一執羽幟相引以為進退之節各皆飲酒朱顏酡鮮挽手連臂合圍歌唱跳舞踴躍得得之聲韻洽齊度通事坐列公廨會眾譁譁

188-1

188. Album on aboriginal customs painted by Chen of Dongning   Qing Dynasty; each picture 34.7 cm long, 29.9 cm wide. This is a picture album depicting the social life of the Gaoshan people in Taiwan in the early stages of the Qing Dynasty. The Gaoshan of Taiwan are members of the Chinese nation. The Gaoshan people and other peoples in Taiwan have opened up, with their hard work, the beautiful and rich island of Taiwan and made great contributions in fighting against foreign aggression, opposing split and separatist regime and safeguarding the unity of China. In early Qing Dynasty, a number of officials and scholars, taking advantage of visits to Taiwan for assuming office or on tour, observed the unique customs of the Gaoshan people. They compiled or wrote books on what they had seen or heard, or asked painters to work on illustrated albums, leaving rich, vivid visual historical material of Taiwan's Gaoshan people in the Qing Dynasty. The aboriginal customs album comprises 70 pages among which are 18 pictures and 24 items reflecting the social customs of the Gaoshan people; 11 illustrations of plants; 3 of animals; and 3 annotations. In the illustrations are many seals bearing Chinese characters reading "Chen of Dongning" or "A River of Spring Water" and so on. Dongning is present-day Taiwan, and Chen would be a Taiwanese. The plates shown are "aboriginal opera," "drink joyfully together," "nose flute" and "capture the wild ox."

聚飲 鼻簫

農事既畢各番互相邀飲必令酒多不拘殽核席地誰呼連角並唇取酒勸飲以為快樂不醉不止鼻簫長可二尺亦有三尺者截竹窾四孔通小孔於竹節之首用鼻吹之管麻連遊戲之具

188-2

捕野牛

番好飼馬不鞍馳驟要捷歡戴輕奇豐草長林屈曲如意擇牝之良者倍價而易以圖孳息內山多野牛民間有購者眾番能乘馬追捕售之價藏熟牛半用未閹生致俟其馴用之

188-3

189-1

189. Gaoshan wooden spoon with human-shaped handle   Qing Dynasty; tableware; 22.5 cm long. The Gaoshan were the earliest inhabitants of Taiwan. Internally they are called Paiwan, Buyi, Taiya or Amei among other names. Wood-carving skill among the Gaoshan is well-developed, some of the most outstanding wood-carvers are Gaoshan, among the ethnic minorities of China. Most brilliant are the ancestral statues and puppets made by the Paiwan people, which are nearly life-sized. On small household articles one frequently sees carvings of human images or snakes. The wooden spoon of the Gaoshan people is used for wine or soup. The shape varies, some in the shape of a melon seed, others round, oval or leaf-shaped.

189-2

190-1

190. Part of ancestral picture of She people Qing Dynasty; full length of the picture 166 cm, width 50 cm. The ancestral picture is also called the "picture of Pan Pao". It contains the images of gods to be used when the She people worship their ancestors. This picture was painted on a piece of white cloth with black, red and green colors in 1759, the 24th year of the Qianlong reign, in Beikong Village, Shisidu, Lishui County, Chuzhou Prefecture, Zhejaing. It depicts the myth and legend of the marriage between the ancestress of the She people and Pan Pao and their descendants. A simple narration appears on every section of the picture. The She people deem the ancestral picture as sacred. At ordinary times, the She people put the portraits and sacrificial utensils, such as the red cloth bag which holds the "ancestral stick" and incense burner, into two bamboo chests in the custody of specially assigned individuals. The picture is unfolded and hung at the time of worshipping the ancestors at Spring Festival, as well as on March 3rd, May 5th, July 15th, August 15th, and December 15th when offerings were placed before the spirit table, and the whole clan would gather together to offer sacrifices in a ceremony presided over by a sorcerer.

190-2

Economy of Early Qing

The ravages of war during the late Ming and early Qing harmed and hindered in varying degrees the development of China's agriculture, handicrafts and commerce, especially in places south of the Yangtze River which were the hardest hit. But as time passed and the flames of war subsided, class and ethnic oppression and contradictions in land-ownership relations became less severe, the human bondage relations of feudal society relaxed, and the burdens of taxation and corvée labor were lightened too. From 1681, the 20th year of Emperor Kangxi's reign, through the reigns of Emperors Yongzheng and Qianlong, the Qing government adopted a series of measures that enabled the social economy to recover gradually and make significant progress, in due time surpassing the highest level of the preceding Ming dynasty.

Agriculture and Water Conservancy

Enlarging the acreage of cultivated land and undertaking water conservancy projects were two basic measures that ensured the recovery and development of agriculture in the Qing Dynasty. To encourage the reclamation of wasteland, the Qing government in its early days summoned people who were unsettled to do this job, alloting to them land, tools, seeds and cattle, and postponing the levying of taxes on the wasteland they reclaimed. When examining the meritorious deeds of local officials, the acreage of land reclaimed was one of the items the government considered. And to encourage landlords and squires to recruit laborers for reclamation of wasteland, the government provided them with favorable terms, such as the levying of taxes on the basis of their returns in land rent. These measures encouraged peasants with no land or only small pieces of land in the Central Plains to migrate to Sichuan, Yunnan and Guizhou provinces and northeastern China, where there were large tracts of virgin land. Thus the area of cultivated land increased continually, exceeding 700 million *mu* (one *mu* = 0.06 hectare) during Emperor Qianlong's reign. The output of farm crops per unit area also increased. More land was devoted to cash crops such as cotton and tobacco. These cash crops, in particular those cultivated in the Yangtze River delta and in the coastal areas of southeastern China, benefited both the tillers and the government. There was also a continuous growth in the country's population, which exceeded 400 million on the eve of the Opium War in 1840. Water conservancy projects to harness the Yellow River and Huai River were undertaken and made fast progress. The projects to harness the rivers through clearing sands with converging flow, and to build the Great Jingjiang Dyke and sea walls in Zhejiang Province, not only increased agricultural production but ensured adequate water transportation.

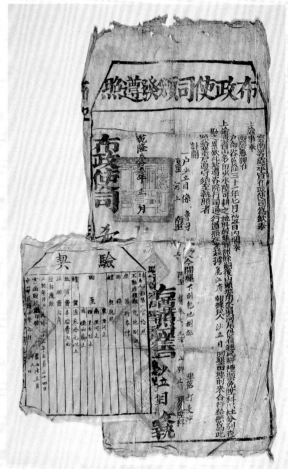

191

191. Reclamation License Relic of Qing, length 52 cm, width 25 cm. The license was issued to Sha Limu by the Administrative Commissioner's Office of Yunnan Province in the first month of the 33rd year (1768) of Emperor Qianlong's reign. On the license is a red seal bearing the characters "Seal of the Lijiang Prefecture." The Qing government encouraged both officials and the people to reclaim wasteland. It ruled that wasteland without owners at the prefecture and county levels, and in areas where troops were stationed, could be cultivated by officers, soldiers, or people with no permanent homes, but wasteland with owners must be reclaimed by the owners themselves. People recruited by local officials from various parts of the country, no matter where they originally lived, were included in the *bao-jia* system (a grassroot administrative structure) of their new homes. And those who reclaimed wasteland were given official licenses with seals, and allowed to work their land indefinitely.

192. Pages from an album on plowing and weaving Paintings by Jiao Bingzhen of the Qing Dynasty, height 24.9 cm.

These are three of a group of paintings depicting agricultural production in the Qing Dynasty. Jiao Bingzhen, a native of Jining (now Jining, Shandong Province), was an official on the Imperial Board of Astronomy. He was skilled in painting human figures and landscapes. This album on plowing and weaving, done during the mid years of Emperor Kangxi's reign, consists of 46 paintings. The emperor appreciated the paintings so much that he ordered craftsmen to carve them on blocks and print them. The pages shown here are on plowing, winnowing and picking mulberry leaves.

192-1

簸揚
臨風細揚簸糠秕凌風
前傾鴻雨聲嘩嘩把玩玉
粒圓短屏箕帚婦收拾
亦已專堂徒戴升斗末
莫倚山年

192-2

株桑
吳兒歌採桑之下有
春深隔生猶崢遠
呼無相漫深籠名年
獨角嚴馬倍尋番鶴
飽紫棋腥覘鳴離拾

192-3

193. Page from an album on catching locusts Painting of Qing. This album was made in 1759, the 24th year of Qing emperor Qianlong's reign, on the orders of Li Yuan, prefect of Huaiyin, Jiangsu Province. He had some artists do the paintings on the basis of experiences in catching locusts. The paintings depicted various ways of exterminating the pests: swatting, luring them with lamps, driving ducks into the fields to eat them, catching them before dawn, trapping them with a reed curtain placed around a big jar, surrounding and killing them in an open space, searching for and digging up nymphs, burying the locusts by turning up the soil, buying and selling locusts. The page reproduced here shows the use of lamps to lure locusts to their destruction. An annotation on the page reads: "All winged insects invariably cluster around flames, and moths often dart into the flames and kill themselves. So lamps should be lit in places where locusts habitually rest, with three or four people keeping watch by each lamp. About a dozen others should be positioned at various points far and near to drive the locusts to the lamps so that the watchers can catch them. The lamps should not be too bright, for a dazzling light may frighten the locusts away and all efforts will be of no avail." This was the best way to catch locusts before midnight. After midnight, or in the hours before dawn, the wings of the insects would be wet with dew and they would not be able to fly very fast or far. By this time, people could catch them without the aid of lamps or other contrivances. Many other methods were used to exterminate locusts during the day. One method was to drive ducks into the fields to eat the locusts. This was an easy way to kill the pests, and it did no damage to the crops. Another method was to place a reed curtain around a big jar. People would stand around on three sides and shoo the insects which, hemmed in by the curtain, would fall into the jar. All these methods were very effective in coping with locusts plagues.

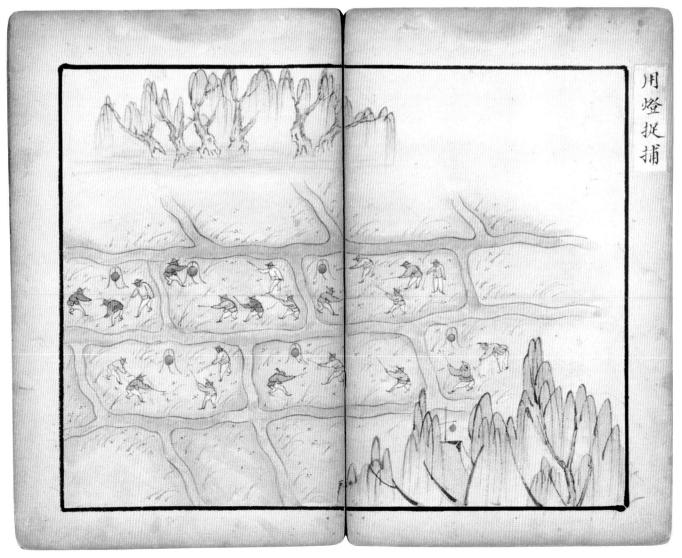

194. Page from a pictorial on building dykes on the Yellow River   Painting of Qing, 30.5 cm x 22 cm. In the early Qing Dynasty, harnessing the Yellow River was an important political and economic issue that had a direct bearing on the national economy and the people's livelihood. Since the Northern Song Dynasty the Yellow River had changed its course, moving south to join the Huai River and together flow into the sea. Of the 1,500 kilometers of the north-south course of the Grand Canal, a stretch of about 100 kilometers formed a part of the Yellow River. When there were floods on the Yellow River or Huai River, transport of grain could be seriously hampered. The pictorial depicts scenes of harnessing the Yellow River in the early Qing.

194-1

194-2

194-3

195. Scroll painting showing the projects undertaken to harness the Huai River (section) Painting by Zhao Cheng of the Qing Dynasty; full length of scroll 543.5 cm, width 46.3 cm. The Huai River and Yellow River caused serious problems to water transportation in the north. In the early Qing, the government attached great importance to harnessing the two rivers, especially at Qingkou and Gaojiayan in Huai'an, where the Yellow River, Huai River and Grand Canal joined. The key projects to harness the Yellow River, dredge the Huai River and clean up the Canal were concentrated in the Qingkou area. So long as the waters of the Canal could move freely, there was no need to worry about transporting grain to the capital by water. This scroll painting depicts in detail the harnessing of rivers during the early Qing.

196. Scroll painting of water conservancy systems in the capital city and its environs (section) Painting by Hongwu of the Qing Dynasty; full length of scroll 1018.3 cm, width 32.9 cm. Hongwu, surnamed Aisin Gioro, styled Zhuoting, also known by the names Nuzhai and Zuiyu, was a member of the Qing imperial clan. He was well-versed in poems and painting. This scroll painting shows the distribution of water systems in and around Beijing during Emperor Qianlong's reign (1736-1795). The scene begins in the Yuquan (Jade Spring) Hill. It shows water flowing down the Western Hills, from where it collects in Kunming Lake, flows into the Chang River, passes through the city and enters the Tonghui and Lu rivers on the southeastern outskirts. The painting also shows water conservancy installations, landscapes, landforms, imperial gardens and city walls in the Beijing area. On the painting are seals with inscriptions that read in translation: "Shiqu Precious Collection," "Precious Collection Rearranged" and "Super Seal of Sanxi Studio." At the end of the scroll are two seals bearing the Chinese characters for "Cheng" (subordinate) and "Wu" (painter's name) and an inscription of 23 lines. The section reproduced here shows Kunming Lake (in what is now the Summer Palace) and other scenes in Beijing.

196-1

Handicrafts

Abolition of the craftsmanship census system in the Qing Dynasty helped promote the development of handicrafts. The major handicraft industry at that time was the textile industry, primarily silk weaving and cotton spinning, with the silk weaving industries of Suzhou, Hangzhou and Nanjing in the lead. Silk weaving also developed rapidly in Foshan, Guangzhou and Sichuan. Cotton textiles not only improved in quality, but increased in quantity and variety, and were being produced in many more places. Besides Songjiang, the cotton textile industries in Wuxi, Suzhou, Nanjing and Foshan all saw fast development.

Porcelain making was a traditional handicraft. During Emperor Qianlong's time, there were more than 40 famous porcelain manufacturing centers in the country. They were found in places under the direct jurisdiction of the imperial court and in the provinces of Jiangsu, Shandong, Anhui, Fujian, Sichuan, Hunan and Guangdong. The most developed porcelain industry was in Jingdezhen, Jiangxi Province, where there were 200-300 non-governmental kilns and well over 100,000 craftsmen, with a precise division of labor that turned out articles of superb workmanship. The techniques of porcelain-firing improved, too. Iron-smelting also saw great progress in the Qing Dynasty. During the Qianlong reign there were several dozen furnaces for making wrought iron and over a hundred for making cast iron in Foshan, Guangdong Province, which turned out a great variety of products. Copper and salt mines in Yunnan, extraction of well salt in Sichuan, tea-processing in Fujian and Yunnan, sugar making in Fujian, Guangdong and Taiwan, paper making in Qianshan and southern Shaanxi, coal mining in Shanxi and Beijing's Mentougou all surpassed in both quantity and quality what the Ming Dynasty had achieved.

197. Cotton cloth Products of Qing. China produced numerous kinds of cloth during the Qing Dynasty. In general, the raw material was cotton or hemp, which was spun into yarn, woven into cloth, then dyed or printed. Blue cotton prints were especially popular. The design or pattern could be white on a blue background or blue on a white background, and the themes could be flowers, figures or legendary tales. One of the two pieces of cloth shown here has a checked pattern; the other, lotus designs. In those days, to make a blue cotton print, designs were first carved on a piece of oilpaper, which was then placed over white cloth. Next, caustic lime and beanpowder were mixed with water to form a dye-resistant paste, which was spread over the paper. When the paste had dried, the paper was removed and the cloth dyed with indigo. After the dye had dried, the paste on the cloth was scraped away and the finished cotton print would appear.

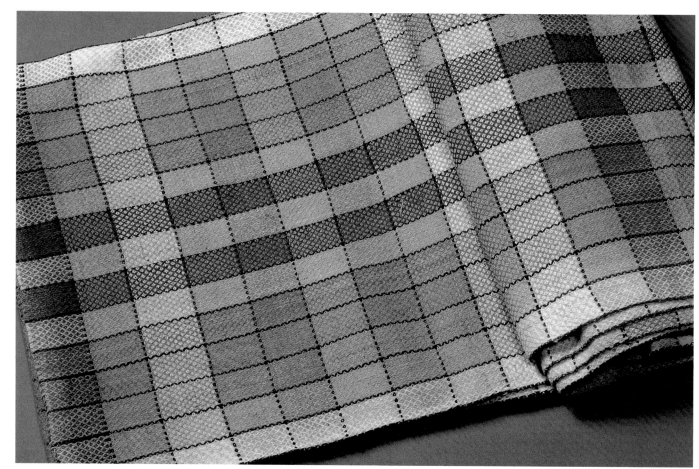

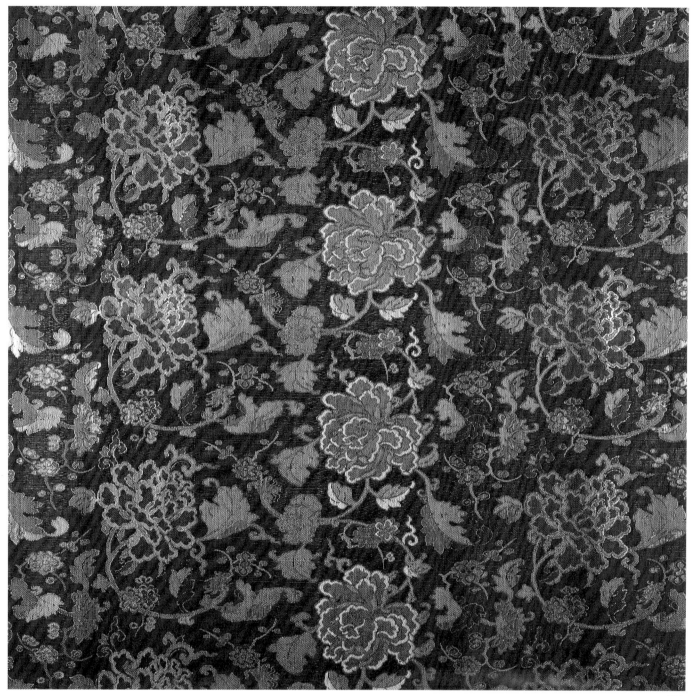

198

198. Gold-thread satin with peony design on blue background Silk fabric of Qing, full length 325 cm, width 79 cm. Satin, named for its satin weave, was silk fabric plain or with designs. It is characterized by wider intervals between the evenly distributed surface dots, which in turn are shaded by the long face threads of the warp and weft on their sides. This makes the fabric smooth and lustrous. The satin shown here was made of high quality silk fabric.

199. Gold-thread satin with cloud-and-dragon design on red background Silk fabric of Qing; full length 686 cm, width 76 cm. It was made for use in the imperial court. The body of the dragon on red satin ground was swively woven by gold thread. Most satin fabrics with dragon designs like this one were woven specially for the imperial court by the Jiangnan Textile Bureau. They were not for the common people.

200-2

200. Large five-color fish bowl Porcelain vessel of Qing, height 25.5 cm, mouth diameter 60 cm. The firing of objects in five colors — red, yellow, blue, green and purple — appeared before the Qing Dynasty. They were overglaze colors and were also called antique colors or strong colors, and were painted on fired white glaze ware, which was then fired a second time. The painting was done in single strong lines, and the colors were heavy and bright, with strong contrasts. The technique reached its zenith during the reign of Emperor Kangxi, which is why five-color porcelains of the Qing Dynasty were also called "Kangxi's five colors." On such five-color porcelains, overglaze blue replaced the underglaze blue of the Ming Dynasty, and black was also used in the overglaze designs. Thus there appeared a kind of porcelain entirely with overglaze colors. The large bowl shown here is a typical Kangxi's five colors.

200-3

200-1

201. Sky blue glazed jar with chrysanthemum design, product of the Kangxi reign Ornament of Qing, height 17.3 cm, mouth diameter 19.1 cm, bottom diameter 15.8 cm. Sky blue glaze made during the Kangxi reign was a kind of colored glaze fired at a high temperature. It was so called because the color was so much like that of the sky. It evolved from light blue with a tinge of green. Its chemical substance contained a little less than 2% cobalt and several other metallic elements such as copper, iron and titanium, all of which were coloring agents that produced a fast and steady glaze color. Most sky blue glazed vessels made during the Kangxi reign were small articles that formed a part of the four treasures of a Chinese study. The jar shown here is a superbly made vessel of the Kangxi reign.

202. Vase with beast-shaped ears, imitation of products of the Guan (official) kilns of the Song Dynasty Ornament of Qing, height 22.3 cm. Guan kilns were under the direct administration of the government, so in terms of craftsmanship their products were always among the best of their time. Of the Guan kilns of different historical periods, those of the Song Dynasty produced articles with the most distinctive features. The kilns in Jingdezhen of the Qing Dynasty made porcelain wares exclusively for the imperial court, so their products were also called Guan kiln products. The vase shown here was made in Jingdezhen during the Qianlong reign (1736-1795) and is an imitation of vases made in Guan kilns of the Song Dynasty. Twin-ear vases appeared at a fairly early date. They were produced in all dynasties since the Sui, but showed much variation in the shapes of the ears: pierced ears, phoenix-shaped ears, ring-shaped ears, fish-shaped ears, etc.

201

203-2

203. Famille-rose openwork vase with a movable core Ornament of Qing, height 30 cm, mouth diameter 8 cm. Famille-rose is an overglaze color that is also called a soft color. It first appeared during the Kangxi reign (1662-1722) and was fully developed during the Yongzheng reign (1723- 1735). It evolved from the five colors (red, yellow, blue, green and purple) by changing their single-line way of painting. Sometimes famille-rose painting was done by applying white frit to the porcelain surface first, then painting the surface in different colors. This openwork vase with a movable core was a new-type vessel first made in the Qing Dynasty. The inner movable core is actually a second vase inside the openwork vase. When it is revolved, different pictures can be seen through the holes in the openwork.

204-2

204-3

204. Sky-clearing blue glazed *haiyan heqing* jar in gold, product of the Qianlong reign Ornament of Qing, height 31.3 cm, mouth diameter 25.1 cm. It was produced in the Jingdezhen imperial kiln for display in Haiyan (Calm Sea) Hall in the Yuanmingyuan (Garden of Perfect Splendor). Sky-clearing blue symbolized *heqing* ("a muddy river is cleared"); the implied meaning is that the world is at peace. Between the neck and shoulders of the jar are two applique ears, molded in the likeness of a pair of swallows with their wings spread and tails scissor-shaped. On the lower part of the belly are three layers of embossed lotus petals in famille rose. The inner wall of the jar and the swallows are glazed in white. The rim of the mouth down to the lower part of the belly on the outer wall are glazed in sky-clearing blue. On the surface of the glaze are plantain leaves and interlocking flowers painted in gold. On the outside bottom of the vase are blue characters in regular script: "Made in the Qianlong reign of the Great Qing." This jar was painted and fired several times, and the workmanship is of very high quality. It is magnificent, dignified, in elegant colors, and exemplifies the best in sculpture, embossing and applique art.

204-1

205-2

205. Plum vase in turquoise green

Ornament of Qing, height 30.1 cm. The vase has a small mouth, short neck, round shoulders, a thin bottom, and a ring foot. The small mouth is suitable for the insertion of plum sprays, hence the name. Quite a lot of plum vases were made in the Song and Yuan dynasties. The blue-and-white plum vases of the Yuan Dynasty made at Jingdezhen possess unique features, but plum vases made in later periods were even more diverse, exquisite and beautiful. Turquoise green glaze, also called sunflower green glaze, first appeared in the Yongzheng reign. The vase shown here belongs to that period.

206. Celestial-body vase with sea-water and posy design in contending colors Ornament of Qing, height 52.2 cm, mouth diameter 11.5 cm, bottom diameter 16.5 cm. A porcelain vessel with a straight mouth, a short neck wider at the top, a big but flat belly, and a slightly concave sandy bottom is called a celestial-body vase. Contending colors refer to the combination of underglaze blue and white with overglaze colors. The first step in making a vase with contending colors is to paint a design in blue and white upon the biscuit, then cover it with glaze. After firing, more colors are added over the glaze to complete the design. This technique first appeared in Jingdezhen during the Xuande reign of the Ming Dynasty and was highly developed during the Chenghua reign. It was further improved during the Yongzheng reign (1723-1735) of the Qing Dynasty, the vase shown here being a typical product of the said period.

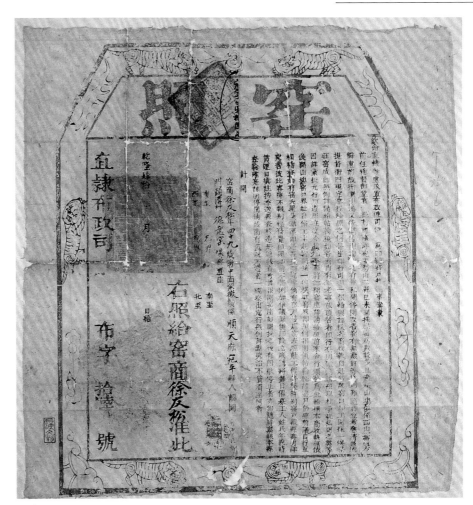

207

206-2

207. Mentougou Coal Pit license Qing relic, 48.3 cm x 45.3 cm. This license was issued to Xu Yousong, a coal pit merchant, by the Administrative Commissioner's Office of Chengxuan, which was under the direct jurisdiction of the imperial court, in 1784, the 49th year of Qianlong's reign. Xu Yousong was a native of Wanping County, Shuntian Prefecture, who operated nongovernmental coal pits. In the early Qing there were many privately owned and operated coal pits at Mentougou in the western suburbs of Beijing. With the passing of time, the costs of mining and transportation became too heavy for the pit owners to bear, for they had to dig deeper and deeper in order to get coal, so they requested permission from the local authorities to shut down the mines. Many pits were closed, production dropped, and the price of coal rose sharply. As this seriously affected the livelihood of the people, Emperor Qianlong on two occasions issued decrees inviting people to invest in coal mining. Before licenses had been issued to prospective investors, the Qing government for a time lost control over the management of the coal mines at Mentougou, which led to the haphazard opening and closing of mines by unscrupulous individuals. The issuance of licenses strengthened the government's control over coal mining. People without a license were not permitted to undertake any mining, while those who had a license could only mine at officially designated places and were not allowed to close pits without permission from the government. The license also stipulated clearly that "if a pit owner illtreats his miners or does not pay them their full wages, other owners may report this to the county government for an investigation." Owners of coal pits were required to keep a muster roll, recording on a day-to-day basis the names of workers employed, their age and appearance, and their native place. The completed rolls had to be sent to the county government quarterly. They were in two copies, one kept by the owner, the other by the government.

Commerce and Emergence of Frontier Cities

The unification of the country and development of agriculture and handicrafts helped promote the prosperity of commerce. Newborn industrial and commercial cities and towns were on the increase. Beijing was not only a political and cultural center at the time, but also a prosperous commercial city. It was where officials and merchants met and goods and products from all parts of the country were assembled. Yangzhou was a distribution center for salt produced in areas along the Huai River. Its economy, too, was well developed. It had a plentiful supply of commodities and was home to many wealthy merchants. Hankou was a distribution center for grain, lumber, medicinal herbs and salt. Located on the middle reaches of the Yangtze River where water transportation was convenient, it was a thriving commercial city. Other cities like Foshan, Guangzhou, Nanjing, Suzhou and Hangzhou were thriving, too. Frontier cities such as Urumqi also flourished. Urumqi was a trade center for nationalities in northern and western China. As a contemporary writer noted, "Merchants from the interior flocked to the city; foreign trade was brisk; goods were assembled there; and the downtown streets were always busy." Towns like Dajianlu (now Kangting County, Sichuan Province) and Duolun were other, newly emerging centers of border trade. Merchants travelled busily among the big cities in those days, and commercial contacts were frequent and numerous. The Qing government set up guest houses to accommodate the merchants. Guest houses for Chinese nationals were called *neiguan* ("domestic hostel"); those for foreigners, *waiguan* ("foreign hostel"). Numerous private banks and pawnshops were opened and currencies were widely circulated. Both land and water transportation developed fast, as grain from the south and cotton from the north were transported in an endless stream through the Grand Canal to various parts of the country.

208

210. Painting of busy street scenes at Qianmen, Beijing The first section of a Qing scroll depicting one of Emperor Qianlong's inspection tours to south China; full length of scroll 2,178 cm, width 72.6 cm. The painting was done by Xu Yang and others in 1776, the 41st year of Qianlong's reign. Xu Yang, a native of Wu County, Jiangsu Province, was good at doing human figures and linear palatial buildings, most of which were for the collection of the Imperial Academy of Art. He was also an official of cabinet rank.

208. Iron sliding weight cast in the 10th year of the Jiaqing reign Weighing apparatus of Qing, height 14.5 cm, width 9.8 cm. On the weight is a hole for inserting a piece of cord and nine characters that mean "official balance, 11th month of the 10th year of the Jiaqing reign." This kind of weighing apparatus has been used for a very long time in China, and is still being used in many small cities, towns and villages today.

209. Ivory ruler Measure of Qing, length 35.5 cm, width 1.9 cm. This was a standard unit of length (equal to 0.32 meter) adopted by the Board of Works of the Qing Dynasty. Its graduations are in 10 *cun* and each *cun* is in 10 *fen*. It was in use for a long time and the graduations on the two ends have worn away.

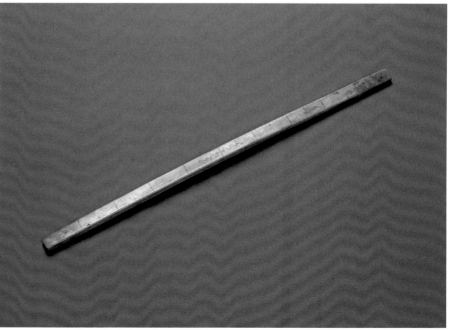

Qing emperors' inspection tours to south China were important political and social activities, the purpose of which was to strengthen ties with landlords and officials of the Han nationality and with scholars and men of letters, keep abreast of public feelings, review and reorganize the army, inspect water conservancy projects on the Yellow and Huai rivers, and check industrial and commercial development. Emperor Qianlong made six inspection tours to south China. They were grand occasions, during which both troops and civilians had to be mobilized. The emperor's retinue included princes, dukes, ministers and other officials as well as imperial guards, totaling over 2,500 people. It was decreed that the tours had to be truthfully represented, in pictures or writing, from the moment the emperor left his capital through the main places and important activities along the way, to his return from the south. This scroll painting is a record of Emperor Qianlong's daily activities during one of his tours. The first section of the painting shows the pomp and ceremony of the emperor's departure from the capital. Straight ahead, outside Zhengyang Gate, is the busy Qianmen Street. Although it is heavily guarded and ordinary people are not allowed to pass through, we see shops in great numbers along both sides of the street, displaying attractive eye-catching signboards. This long scroll is of great historical value, casting light on local scenes, customs and habits, as well as the prosperity of the capital's economy and culture.

210-1

211

211. Signboard of Puji Pawnshop   Wooden signboard of Qing Dynasty, 33 cm high, 48 cm wide, 3.5 cm thick. On the board is a bronze loop handle for hanging. Its four corners are protected by bronze triangles with cloud designs. The two upper corners are slightly bent. On the front of the board is the name of the shop — Puji Pawnshop — and on the back is the Chinese character for "pawn", all in bronze inlay. The Chinese character for "pawn" was a common sign on signboards of pawnshops in the Ming and Qing dynasties. This pawnshop, located in Taigu County, Shanxi Province, was opened during the Daoguang reign (1821-1850) of the Qing Dynasty and remained in business until shortly before 1949. Pawnshops in those days gave high-interest loans, accepting clothes and other articles as security. Their names were related to Buddhist doctrines, such as *puji* ("universal salvation") and *huiji* ("benefit all"). The front of a pawnshop was set up in a special way. There was always a screen behind the front door, so that outsiders could not see what was going on inside. It offered some consolation to people who came to the shop to pawn their valuables.

212. Two pictures from an album on Beijing's shop fronts   Qing relics. Architectural styles of shops in Beijing were very much alike during the Qing Dynasty, yet each shop had its special features. The front

212-1

212-2

of a shop was gorgeously decorated and showed the shop's name. Dealers in refreshments, soaps, shoes, hats, knives or scissors all had their own way of decorating their establishment. The pictures reproduced here show the fronts of the Xingfa Noodle Shop and Wang Mazi's Scissors Shop.

213. Scroll painting depicting the transport of grain to the capital through the Tonghui Canal (section) Painting by Shen Yu, Qing Dynasty; full length of scroll 346.7 cm, width 42.2 cm. The painting depicts the transport of grain to the capital through the Tonghui Canal during the Kangxi reign of the Qing Dynasty. Tonghui Canal, also called Datong Canal and Capital Grain Transport Canal, was dug in 1291, the 28th year of the Zhiyuan reign of the Yuan Dynasty. It was designed and built by Guo Shoujing and extended from Dadu (now Beijing) to Tongzhou. Through this canal, boats transporting grain from the south could reach Jishuitan inside Beijing. It was repeatedly dredged and repaired in the Ming and Qing dynasties, during which it continued to be used. Later, however, palace walls were built over parts of the canal, so that boats carrying grain had to anchor at the Datong Bridge in the southeastern outskirts of the city. Confronted with the problem of diminishing water resources, the Qing government dispensed with the use of the many locks on the canal. Instead, workers were hired to carry grain from the grain boats to other boats moored at upper levels of the canal. This situation is vividly and accurately portrayed in the scroll painting.

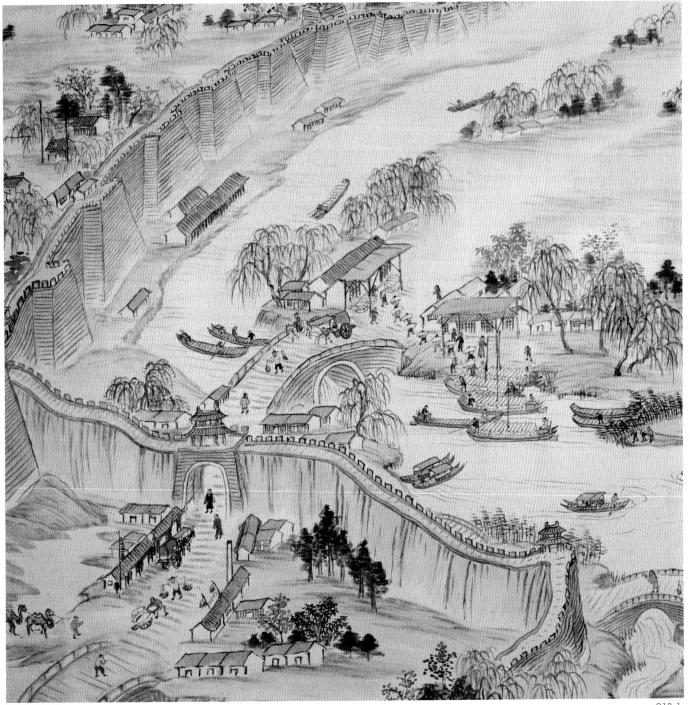

213-1

Economic and Cultural Exchange between China and Other Countries in the Early Qing

In its early days, the Qing government adopted a closed-door policy, strictly controlling foreign trade and people-to-people commercial exchange. It was not until 1682, the 21st year of Kangxi's reign, when the Qing had reunited Taiwan with the rest of the country that restrictions on overseas trade were relaxed and Guangzhou, Zhangzhou,Ningpo and Yuntaishan (now Lianyungang, Jiangsu Province) were opened as trade ports. In 1720, the 59th year of Kangxi's reign, *gonghang* (a foreign trade administration) was set up. At that time Chinese silk, tea and porcelain were being exported in large quantities; and European commodities such as watches, clocks and woollen goods had found their way to China. Qing's relations with neighboring Korea and Japan further developed; government envoys were often dispatched on mutual visits, while nongovernmental interchanges and commercial activities became increasingly frequent. China also maintained economic and cultural exchanges with Vietnam, Cambodia, India and southwestern Asian countries. Scientific instruments from the West were introduced into China, boosting the development of China's science and technology.

Sketch Map of Foreign Trade Ports in the Early Qing Dynasty

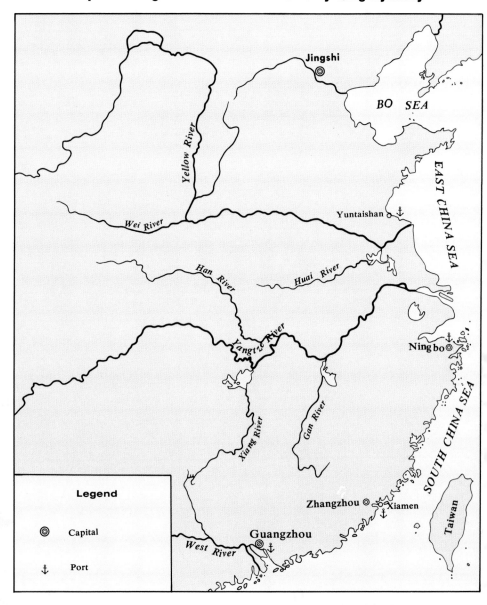

214

214. Korean blue and white vase with cloud-and-dragon design Imported in the Qing Dynasty; height 51.6 cm, mouth diameter 17.5 cm, bottom diameter 18 cm. In the early Qing, China and Korea conducted regular trade fairs on their borders and Korean commodities were imported into China in large quantities. Korean blue and white porcelain wares were brought to China not only as commodities but often as gifts.

215. Korean colored writing paper Imported in the Qing Dynasty. Relations between China and Korea were further developed in the Qing Dynasty. Thanks to its fine long fibers, Korean paper is tough and very popular among the Chinese people. People in northeastern China often paste it on windows to keep their rooms warm. In former times, Korean paper was often introduced into China through border trade or as gifts.

215

216. Japanese pen holder with landscape design traced in gold on black lacquer ground Gift to the Qing court from Japan; height 22.8 cm, mouth and bottom diameter both 21.2 cm. Tracing a design in gold on lacquer ground is called "transplant painting" in Japan. The technique was introduced from China, but Japanese artists improved on it so that their technique has surpassed China's in some respects. During the Ming and Qing dynasties, large numbers of Japanese gold lacquer wares and lacquer wares with designs in gold were brought to China. The pen holder shown here is an exquisitely made Japanese article.

217. Japanese enamel vase with wild chrysanthemum and flying birds design made by *qibao* Gift to the Qing imperial court from Japan; height 47.5 cm, mouth diameter 13 cm, bottom diameter 14 cm. *Qibao* ("seven treasures"), also called *qibaoshao* ("firing seven treasures"), is a Japanese traditional craft. The body of the object is made of some precious metal. It is decorated with material that is mostly quartz and includes different color pigments and is then fired. The technique is similar to the Chinese metal-body enamel craft. According to the method of production, *qibaoshao* may be divided into two kinds: *qibaoshao* with wire and *qibaoshao* without wire. *Qibaoshao* with wire is akin to enameling with filigree, which is similar to Chinese cloisonné, but the raw material and materials for making enamel used in Japan have their special features. *Qibaoshao* without wire is a way of producing painted enamel. The enamel is coated directly on the metal body. After firing, colors appear that are very much like paint. The finished object is like Chinese painted enamel, but Japanese *qibaoshao* without wire is executed on a thinner body, and the glaze surface is smooth and lustrous like glass. The vase shown here is an example of *qibaoshao* without wire.

217-1

216

217-2

218. Two bottles of Italian snuff   Gifts to the Qing government from Italy; height 23.8 cm. China's contacts with foreign countries increased considerably in the late Ming and early Qing dynasties. People from military and political circles in the West came to China in an endless stream. Christian missionaries, merchants, journalists and sinologists also came to engage in various activities; some even accepted posts in the Qing government.

218

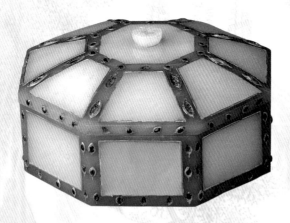

219

219. Box inlaid with blue and white jade   Gift to the Qing government from Hindustan; height 6.8 cm, mouth and bottom diameter both 13.3 cm. The box is inlaid with pieces of blue and white jade. Hindustan was located in an area covering parts of what are now northwestern India, northern Pakistan and eastern Afghanistan, where jade was found in abundance and the jade carving industry prospered. After Qing emperor Qianlong put down rebellions north and south of the Tianshan Mountains, large numbers of jade articles of Hindustani origin were introduced into China. Emperor Qianlong was very fond of these works of art in exotic styles. He collected them in great numbers and composed poems and essays praising them.

220. Iron slotting tool with gold design
Gift to Qing emperor Qianlong from king of Nepal; length 40.3 cm. The gift was presented to the Qing emperor in 1785, the 50th year of Qianlong's reign. Between 1767 and 1768, the chief of Gurkha, after conquering three small regimes of the Malla Dynasty in the Nepal valley, established the state of Nepal. In the course of expanding its territory, Nepal twice sent troops to invade Tibet, but was driven out by the Qing army which pursued the invaders into Nepal. The Nepalese government sued for peace, and later became a vassal state paying tributes to the Qing court.

220

221

221. Gold medal Gift to Qing emperor Qianlong from Burma; perimeter 115 cm. Burma is a neighboring country of China. Over the past two thousand years, the two countries have established close ties with each other. In 1753, the 18th year of Emperor Qianlong's reign, the king of Burma sent envoys with large numbers of gifts to China to boost friendly relations. The envoys were accorded a grand reception by the Qing government. Later, because of warfare, relations between the two countries were suspended. They were renewed during the last years of Qianlong's reign and trade activities, too, were resumed.

222. Elephant tusks Gift to the Qing government from Vietnam; length 150 cm, upper end diameter 12 cm. In 1660, the 17th year of the Shunzhi reign, the king of Vietnam sent envoys to Beijing. The two governments presented gifts to each other, enhancing their mutual understanding. Trade between China and Vietnam flourished, too. Chinese junks loaded with porcelain, silk and satin sailed to Vietnam; gold, silver and other minerals, as well as ivory were continually transported from Vietnam into China.

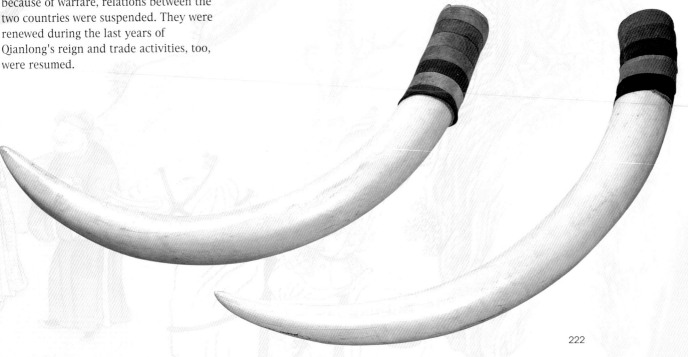

222

223. Silver bowl with design in relief, depicting the tale of a golden deer   Gift presented to the Qing government from Combodia in the 18th century; height 13.5 cm, mouth diameter 19 cm, bottom diameter 14 cm. Cambodia abounds in historical tales, legends and myths. Some of the best known are "The Tale of a Banded Krait," "A Tale of Thunder and Lightning," "Tales of Mosquitoes," and "The Tale of a Golden Deer," which is the theme of the design on this silver bowl.

223-1

224. Paintings of aliens from France and England   From a Qing pictorial album *Guang Yu Sheng Lan.* After finishing an album entitled *Tributes Paid by Vassal States,* Jin Tingbiao and others were ordered by the Qing government to produce a handwritten copy and a printed edition of their album. A copy of *Guang Yu Sheng Lan* was also made. It differed from the copy of *Tributes Paid by Vassal States* in that all the inscriptions in Manchu were omitted; only inscriptions in the Han language were retained. Paintings of aliens were still placed at the beginning of the album; the two shown here are of French and English people in the 18th century.

225. Saberlike waist knife with jasper inlaid handle and leather sheath   Gift to Qing emperor Qianlong from George Macartney, a British envoy; length 97.7 cm. In 1792, the 57th year of Qianlong's reign, G. Macartney led a British mission to China. He arrived in Beijing the following year. Emperor Qianlong received him on two occasions in Wanshu Garden of his imperial palace in Chengde north of the capital. G. Macartney put forward seven demands, including stationing an envoy in Beijing, opening ports for trade, reducing customs duty and freedom of missionary work, all of which were rejected by the Qing government. Shortly afterward he returned to England by boat through the Grand Canal via Hangzhou and Guangzhou, taking with him a letter and gifts from Emperor Qianlong to the Queen of England.

224-1

224-2

225-1

225-2

226

228. Famille-rose water purification bottle with yellow background

Relic of Qing; height 22.5 cm, mouth diameter 7.2 cm, bottom diameter 10 cm. The bottle, an export commodity of the Qing Dynasty, was used by religious believers. It has a nipplelike spout between the neck and belly, which is big and round. Most such bottles were produced in Jingdezhen, Jiangxi Province, during the Ming and Qing dynasties.

226. Underglaze blue-and-white plate with pavilion design

Relic of Qing; height 4.2 cm, rim diameter 21.5 cm, base diameter 13.1 cm. Underglaze blue-and-white is also called underglaze blue or blue design under white glaze. The designs are clear, and the colors fast and stable. Porcelain wares of this kind were a major variety of the ceramic exports of the Qing Dynasty, and were very popular in Southeast Asia and other regions. The porcelain plate shown here was an export article.

227. Underglaze blue-and-white bowl with human figures bearing the name of its producer, Yongyuancheng Ji

Relic of Qing; height 13.2 cm, rim diameter 22.1 cm, base diameter 9.7 cm. An export commodity of the Qing Dynasty. Among the large number of Qing porcelain for export, a certain proportion bore the names of workshops where the vessels were made. Porcelain wares produced at Yongyuancheng Ji sold well both at home and abroad; they were highly commercialized.

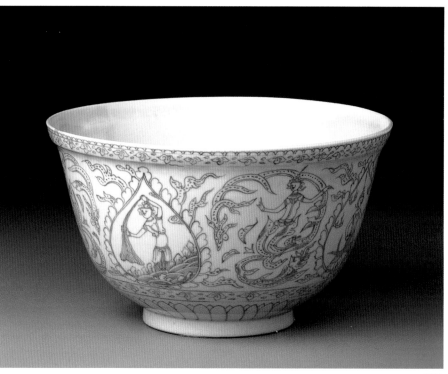

227

Science and Culture

Quite a few progressive thinkers, famous scientists, novelists, calligraphers, painters and handicraftsmen emerged in the Qing Dynasty. Many of them were able to create new works or new ideas on the basis of the achievements of their predecessors; some accepted Western ideas in science and technology. Their accomplishments added a new chapter to the history of Chinese science and culture before the modern era.

Science and Technology

Social and economic progress in the Qing Dynasty and the introduction of Western knowledge of science and technology further promoted the development of natural science in China. The most outstanding achievements were in astronomy, the calendar and mathematics. The Chinese mathematicians Mei Wending and Ming Antu, and astronomer Wang Xichan made notable discoveries during their studies. The Qing Dynasty also saw new progress in the medical field, including clinical disciplines and pharmacology.

trigonometric functions in power series, which was proven by his discovery of the "Ratio for Determining Segment Areas," thus pushing the study of trigonometric functions and π to a new level. Another celebrated mathematician of the Qing Dynasty was Mei Wending (1633-1721). In the *Summary of Master Mei's Series* alone, there are 13 categories, totaling 40 volumes, of his mathematic works. He was a man with many new ideas, conceived through independent thinking. He introduced European knowledge of mathematics into China.

230. *Illustrations and Explanations of Implements Used in Water Conservancy Projects* Written by Lin Qing of the Qing Dynasty. The book describes implements used in water conservancy projects, especially those related to river control. It consists of two parts, published in four volumes based on the needs of different engineering projects, such as flood prevention, dredging, emergency measures for protecting embarkments. Each implement is provided with an illustration accompanied by textual explanations. The book is also a scientific summary of experiences in water conservancy of the Qing Dynasty.

229

229. *Quick Method for Determining Segment Areas* A four-volume mathematic work by Ming Antu of the Qing Dynasty. Ming Antu (1692-1765), styled Jing'an, was a native of the Zhengbai Banner, Mongolia (today's southern Xilin Gol, Inner Mongolia Autonomous Region). After making a detailed study of the important achievements of Western mathematicians, he wrote a book that fully confirmed the nine formulae of infinite series, including expressions of trigonometric functions in power series and an expression of the nth power of π, opening a new channel for the study of trigonometric functions and π by analytic methods. He also developed a new formula for trigonometric functions and inverse

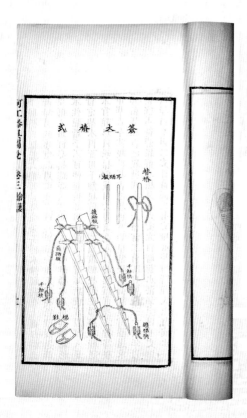

231

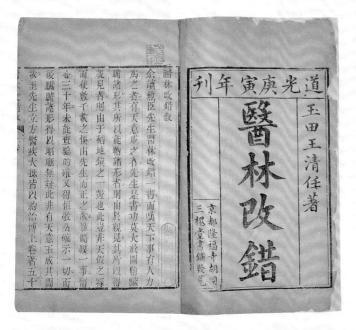

231. *Errors in Medicine Corrected* **(in two volumes)** By Wang Qingren of the Qing Dynasty. Wang Qingren (1768-1831) was a native of Yutian (in today's Hebei Province). He began to study medicine at about 20, and soon found that there were errors on the structure and functions of internal organs of the human body in ancient medical books. Based on his own observations, he drew a picture titled "Human Internal Organs As I See Them" and put it together with pictures of internal organs drawn by the ancients in the forepart of his work *Errors in Medicine Corrected,* to help others make comparative studies. His knowledge of the internal organs of the human body was indeed much better than his predecessors. He laid stress on the importance of understanding internal organs to a doctor in curing diseases, that is, the importance of linking medicine to the anatomical physiology of the human body. His medical theory was based on knowledge of human body anatomy. He listed, as examples, 20 cases of deficiency of vital energy and 50 cases of blood stasis, and prescribed 30 new remedies, making new contributions to the development of traditional Chinese medicine.

232. Back massage manipulator Medical instrument of Qing; length 14.1 cm, width 13 cm. This manipulator was a physical therapy instrument used for massage in the Qing imperial palace. The handle is made of jade; the beads are made of amethyst and agate, and they revolve on a gilded axle. Rolling the instrument over the clothed body can relieve pain in the muscles and promote the circulation of blood and vital energy in the whole body or any part of it. It helps to relax the muscles and stimulate blood circulation, reinforces the effects of medicine and achieves results that medicine can not produce.

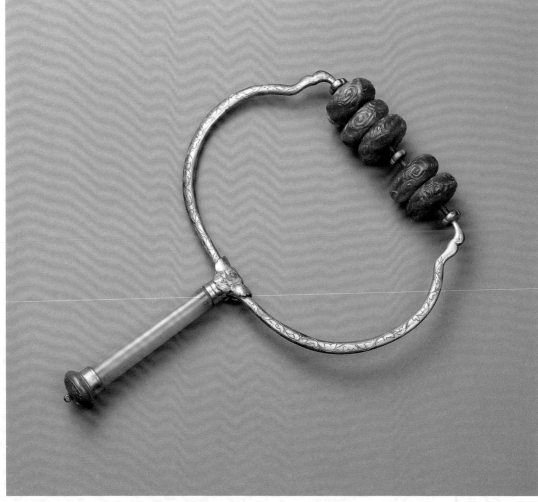

233-1

233. Celestial globe made by Qi Yanhuai

Relic of Qing. Qi Yanhuai (1774-1841), styled Meilu, was a native of Wuyuan (in present-day Jiangxi Province). A scientist of the mid-Qing Dynasty, he made outstanding contributions to the study of astronomy and farm irrigation. This celestial globe, based on an astronomical timing instrument, was made by Qi Yanhuai in 1830, the 10th year of the Daoguang reign. Its internal mechanism is like that of a clock, using a spring as the motive power. It tells the time automatically. In ancient China, ways of telling time — year, month, date, hour— were all related to astronomy and inseparable from astronomical phenomena. Wang Xichan (1628-1682), another celebrated astronomer of the Qing Dynasty, made important contributions to the expounding of such phenomena. He was the author of the book *The Surviving Works of Xiao'an*. In his theory of the movements of celestial bodies, he showed for the first time how to calculate the initial contacts of solar and lunar eclipses and the angular positions of the last contacts.

Philosophy

During the late Ming and early Qing three eminent philosophers, Huang Zongxi, Gu Yanwu and Wang Fuzhi, honored as the "three masters," appeared in China. Their philosophical ideas were basically materialist, and their political thinking was democratic. They were men of great learning, each of whom achieved notable success in his way and made outstanding contributions that had a far-reaching influence on the academic world of later generations.

234-1

234-2

234. Portrait of Huang Zongxi and a page from *A Ming Barbarian Waiting for a Visitor*   Huang Zongxi (1610-1695), styled Taichong, also called Lizhou and Nanlei, was a native of Yuyao (in today's Zhejiang Province). He was a celebrated thinker of the late Ming and early Qing. When Qing armies marched south to attack the Ming, Huang organized resistance against the invaders in eastern Zhejiang Province. After his efforts failed, he retired into seclusion and wrote books. He was opposed to the "reason first, vitality second" theory of the Neo-Confucianism of the Song Dynasty, believing that "reason is one with vitality; without vitality, there can be no reason." This is rudimentary materialist thinking, which teaches that spirit is determined by matter. His political thinking had a tinge of democracy as opposed to feudalist autocracy. He held the view that "order or disorder in a country depends on the happiness or sorrow of the masses rather than the rise or fall of one family." He advocated "universal laws" to replace the emperor's "family laws." He also put forward the view that "both industry and commerce are essentials," which represented the interests and demands of the newly emerging stratum of townspeople at a time when commodity economy was on the rise. *A Ming Barbarian Waiting for a Visitor* is his representative work.

235. Portrait of Gu Yanwu and a page from his *Daily Accumulated Knowledge* Gu Yanwu (1613-1682), styled Ningren, also known as Tinglin, was a native of Kunshan (in today's Jiangsu Province). He was a famous thinker and scholar of the late Ming and early Qing.   When Qing armies marched south to attack the Ming, he organized the people in his native place to resist the invaders. When his cause failed, he left home and went on a long journey to explore distant mountains, rivers and other geographical conditions. He read extensively and did research on the Confucian classics, history, astronomy, geography, phonology, and epigraphy. He was a materialist philosopher, believing that the universe was formed of matter, that it was matter in a state of changing motion. He opposed feudalist autocratic monarchy, holding that "every individual is responsible for the rise and fall of his country." In his academic pursuits, he was opposed to empty talk, advocating that learning should be for the purpose of utilization, and that every effort should be made to solve practical problems in the nation's economy and the people's livelihood. *Daily Accumulated Knowledge,* one of his major works, is a collection of his reading notes. It expounds what the author gained from his study of the Confucian classics, of the administration of local officials, and of finance and taxes, laws and institutions, geography, literature and fine arts; it delves deep into these subjects; and corrects the errors and deviations in them.

236. Portrait of Wang Fuzhi and his *Nightmare* Wang Fuzhi (1619-1692), styled Ernong, also known as Jiangzhai, was a native of Hengyang (in today's Hunan Province). He was an outstanding thinker of the late Ming and early Qing. When Qing armies invaded the south, he actively engaged in resisting the invaders. After the failure of his cause, he retired into seclusion and buried himself in writing. He was also called "Master Chuanshan" because in his late years he lived at the foot of Shichuanshan (Mt. Shichuan) in Hengyang. Academically, he inherited and developed the materialist thought of Zhang Zai of the Song Dynasty. Through criticism of both subjective and objective idealism, which had emerged in the Ming and Qing dynasties, and sorting out all that was good in ancient

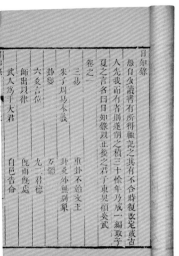

235-2

235-1

materialism, he put forward materialist theories that were sounder than those of any of his predecessors. He was the first to affirm that the universe was formed of *qi,* or "vitality," an objective reality. *Qi,* he asserted, is matter in a state of changing motion; it may gather and disperse, come and go, but it can never be extinguished; and thus the world is a material body in which matter is primary and inextinguishable. In epistemology, he held that knowledge originates from things that exist objectively, not from man's subjective thinking. He also believed that things are constantly changing and in human society there can be no comparison between past and present. He wrote many books; *Nightmare* is one of them.

236-1

236-2

Leishu (encyclopedia) and *Congshu* (collection of books)

A *leishu* is a comprehensive reference work with entries arranged by subject matter or by some conventional method such as number of strokes or radicals like a dictionary. Examples are the *Collected Works on Literature and the Fine Arts*, *Notes of the First Learning*, and *The Taiping Imperial Encyclopedia* compiled during the Tang and Song dynasties. A large-sized *leishu*, the *Yongle Encyclopedia*, was compiled during the Ming, and it was followed by the largest and most comprehensive of all *leishu*, *An Encyclopedia of Ancient and Modern Books* published during the reign of Qing emperor Kangxi. A *congshu* differs from a *leishu* in that it is a collection of books related in some way that are published as a series. The contents of the books are not rearranged according to subject matter but are presented in their original order as independent works. *The Complete Library in Four Divisions* compiled during the Qing is an example. A *leishu* is more convenient to the study of special subjects while a *congshu* provides a more complete source of information.

237

237. *Encyclopedia of Ancient and Modern Books* This is the biggest encyclopedia extant in China. It was compiled during Qing emperor Kangxi's reign under the guidance of Chen Menglei, a successful candidate in the highest imperial examination. By the order of Prince Cheng, 3rd son of Emperor Kangxi, Cheng Menglei started compiling the book in 1700 and the first draft was ready in 1706, six years later. After another ten years the manuscript was submitted to Emperor Kangxi for approval. The emperor gave it the title *Encyclopedia of Ancient and Modern Books* and asked some scholars to go over the manuscript again. During the Yongzheng reign, Jiang Tingxi and some others reexamined the manuscript and finalized it after making some additions and deletions and polishing the text. The book in its final form consisted of six

238-2

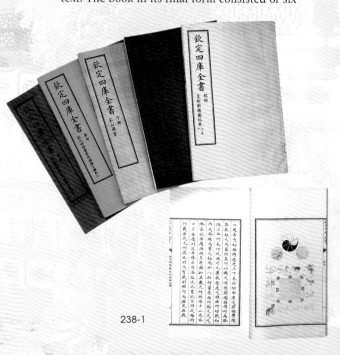

238-1

major parts: calculation of the movements of heavenly bodies, the earth, ethics, nature study, study of Confucian classics and economy. It divided into 32 categories, 6,109 sections, 10,000 volumes and publishd in 5,000 copies.

238. *The Complete Library in Four Divisions* and portrait of Ji Yun

The *Complete Library in Four Divisions* is a large collection of books compiled during Qing emperor Qianlong's reign. In 1773, the imperial court set up a publishing house called the Complete Library in Four Divisions, with Ji Yun as editor-in-chief. Ji Yun (1724-1805) was a native of Xian County (in today's Hebei Province). Compilation of the book was completed in 1781. It collected 3,503 titles in 79,337 volumes. To make it easier to read, the contents were copied neatly by hand. Altogether seven handwritten copies were made, in addition to a master copy. These were stored in four pavilions in the inner chambers of the imperial palace and three pavilions in Zhejiang Province. The *Complete Library in Four Divisions* collected as many titles as were available at the time, published or unpublished. Many were rare or privately owned works, in which very valuable historical documents were preserved. Incidentally, the name *Complete Library in Four Divisions* originated in the reign of Emperor Xuanzong of Tang when four archives were set up in the country's two capitals to preserve books in the four categories of Confucian classics, history, philosophy and literature.

239. *The Twenty-Four Dynastic Histories*

Publications of the Qing Dynasty. In ancient China, histories of all dynasties were compiled as legacies for later generations. During the Qing emperor Qianlong's reign, after the *History of the Ming Dynasty* was completed, the emperor ordered the compilation and publication of the histories of all past dynasties in biographical style. Altogether, 24 histories were compiled and published, collectively entitled *The Twenty-Four Dynastic Histories*. The individual titles were *Records of the Historian, Book of the Han Dynasty, Book of the Later Han Dynasty, Book of the Three Kingdoms, Book of the Jin Dynasty, Book of the Song Dynasty, Book of the Southern Qi Dynasty, Book of the Liang Dynasty, Book of the Chen Dynasty, Book of the Wei Dynasty, Book of the Northern Qi Dynasty, Book of the Zhou Dynasty, Book of the Sui Dynasty, History of the Southern Dynasties, History of the Northern Dynasties, Old History of the Tang Dynasty, New History of the Tang Dynasty, Old History of the Five Dynasties, New History of the Five Dynasties, History of the Song Dynasty, History of the Liao Dynasty, History of the Jin Dynasty, History of the Yuan Dynasty,* and *History of the Ming Dynasty.*

239

Novels and Traditional Operas

In Qing literature, major achievements were made in the area of novels and traditional operas. The best-known novels are *Strange Tales from Liaozhai, The Scholars, A Dream of Red Mansions,* etc. Among traditional operas, a new kind of opera— Peking Opera — appeared.

240

240. *The Scholars* by Wu Jingzi   This is a long novel satirizing the imperial examination system. Wu Jingzi (1701-1754) was a native of Chuanjiao (in today's Chuanjiao County, Anhui Province). Born in a declining bureaucrat family, he was a poor scholar who failed to pass the imperial examination. He moved to Nanjing later, and made a living by writing. His novel *The Scholars,* focusing on the problems of fame and wealth, describes scholars of all types, praising upright intellectuals who did not seek riches and glory, and exposing scholars of loose conduct who sought to pass the imperial exams merely to win fame and fortune and eventually degenerated into corrupt officials, local tyrants or evil gentry.

241. Album on *Strange Tales from Liaozhai*   This album of paintings by Qing artists is based on Pu Songling's *Strange Tales from Liaozhai.* Pu Songling (1640-1715), a Mongol whose home was in Zichuan (now Zibo, Shandong Province), was a celebrated man of letters of the Qing Dynasty. *Strange Tales from Liaozhai* is a collection of his best short stories. Using tales of ghosts, fox fairies and dreams, the author exposed the darkness of social reality in his time and expressed the longings of the people for a happy life.

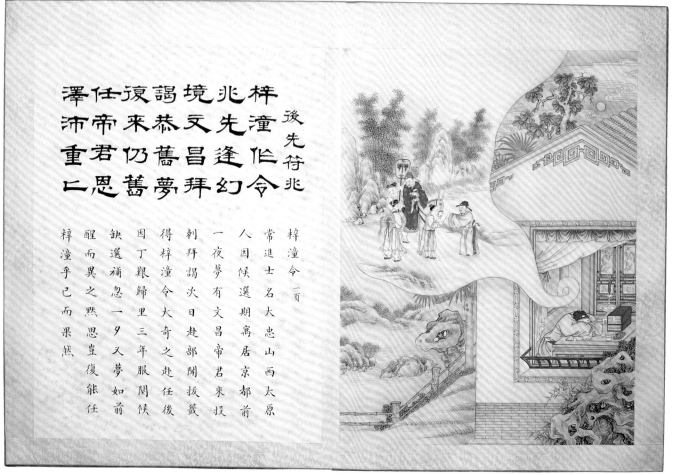

241-1

242

242. *A Dream of Red Mansions* A long novel by Cao Xueqin (1724-1764), a realistic man of letters of the Qing Dynasty. Cao, a Manchu, lived during China's last feudal dynasty. The rise and fall of his clan greatly changed his life and thinking. These vicissitudes provided the source material for his writings and led to the completion of this great novel of realism. Centering on four great families — Jia, Shi, Wang and Xue— that were closely connected by marriages over several generations, the author described their declining fortunes, through which he sensed that the whole feudal system was in its death throes. *A Dream of Red Mansions* is a novel of high aesthetic quality among Chinese classical novels and occupies a prominent place in the history of world literature. The extant version of the novel is in 120 chapters, of which 80 chapters were written by Cao Xueqin himself and the last 40 chapters completed by another writer, Gao E, after Cao's death.

243. Painting of the Grand View Garden Scroll painting on paper, height 137 cm, width 362 cm. The painting is a scene of the Grand View Garden, a venue frequented by Jia Baoyu and Lin Daiyu, the hero and heroine of *A Dream of Red Mansions*. It shows five buildings in different architectural styles — the Alpinia Garden, Concave Crystal Lodge, Smartweed Breeze Cot, Peony Pavilion and Convex Emerald Mountain Villa — and in their midst the images of 173 characters from the novel. The painting was done by a folk artist of the Qing Dynasty; its style is close to that of a woodcut. It is a piece of valuable material for the study of *A Dream of Red Mansions*.

243-1

243-2

243-3

趙雲

孔明

魯素

244. Female stage costume of red satin with colored embroidery and gold-thread woven design Product of Shengping Shu (a bureau in charge of theatrical performances in the Qing imperial palace). Peking Opera was the last theatrical form to evolve from ancient Chinese local operas. Its performing art inherited the traditional ways of singing and dancing. Singing, reciting, acting and acrobatics are the performing mediums of Peking Opera, of which "acting" is a general term for body movements on the stage and "acrobatics" refers to the dance movements of traditional martial arts. These mediums are governed by fixed rules, which are generally referred to as "stylized movements." Roles in the Peking Opera are generally classified into four types: *sheng* (male role), *dan* (female role), *jing* (painted face, subdivided into civilian painted face and warrior painted face) and *chou* (clown). The traditional stage costumes of Peking Opera are based on costumes of the Ming Dynasty. Ceremonial robes embroidered with dragons are worn by emperors and senior officials on the stage. The colors of a robe indicate the rank of the wearer; yellow is the most distinguished color, and is used exclusively by the emperor. The costume shown here was for female roles staged in the Qing imperial palace.

Handicraft Articles and Paintings

Handicraft articles of the Qing Dynasty were rich and colorful. Painted enamel wares with bronze bodies made in Kangxi's reign, jade articles and bamboo wares of Qianlong's reign were exquisite works of art. First-rate painters emerged one after another, notably the "four Wangs" (Wang Shimin, Wang Jian, Wang Hui and Wang Yuanqi) and "four monks" (Hongren, Kuncan, Yuanji and Zhu Da) of the early Qing, and Zheng Xie, celebrated painter of the mid-Qing.

245. Blue jade twin-washer decorated with six dragonflies and rings

Ornament of the Qing Dynasty; height 6.3 cm, greatest width of mouth 15.4 cm, distance between legs 6.72 cm. Jade carvings of the Qing Dynasty were of remarkable workmanship. The Qing imperial court set up a handicraft department, under which were jade-carving workshops engaged in recruiting craftsmen from all parts of the country to carve jade articles for imperial use. As to jade-carving workshops owned by the common people, the ones in Beijing, Yangzhou, Suzhou and Dali were the most famous. The raw material used in jade-carving was jadeite in white, blue, green, yellow or emerald, and the most commonly seen jade articles were vases, bottles, bowls, washers and flower receptacles, as well as images of animals and miniature hills of relatively large size. The twin-washer shown here consists of two square washers joined at two corners. At each of the six free corners stands a carved dragonfly holding a jade ring in its mouth. The pattern is simple, dignified and unique.

246. Bamboo tube carved with a design of five ghosts creating a fuss on judgement day

Vessel for perfuming, Qing relic; height 21 cm, mouth diameter 4 cm. Bamboo carving saw great progress during the Ming and Qing dynasties; there were carvings in bas-relief, high relief, openworks, raised patterns, incised patterns, threadlike carvings, etc. Nanjing and Jiading were especially famous for their jade carvings. The usual process was first to paint a design in ink on the bamboo, then to carve along the ink lines. Jade articles were of two major categories, one for practical use, the other for decoration. Regarding the five ghosts carved on the article shown here, there are different interpretations. Some say that the five were wicked ghosts who had no wit, no learning, no literary taste, no luck and no social communication. In the Tang Dynasty people believed that the five ghosts referred to Chen Jue, Feng Yansi, Feng Yanlu, Wei Cen and Cha Wenhui, who colluded with each other in doing wicked things. In the Song Dynasty, however, the five ghosts were believed to be the treacherous Wang Qinruo, Ding Wei, Lin Te, Chen Pengnian and Liu Chenggui.

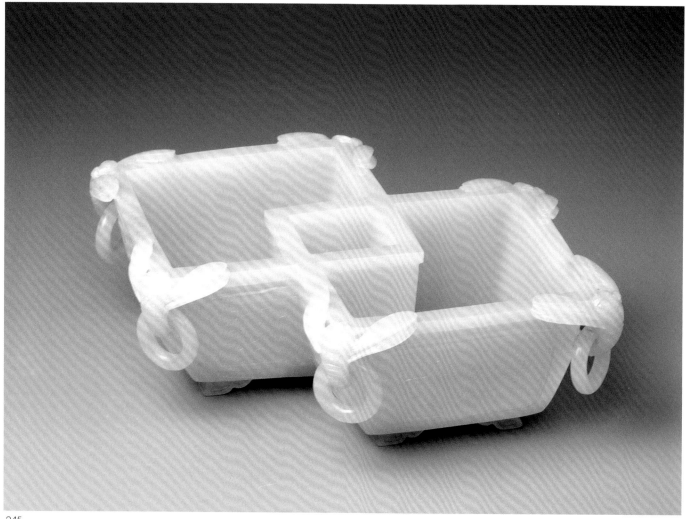

245

246 ▷

247-3

247. Bamboo brush holder with design "Liu Hai Plays with a Golden Toad" Stationery carved by Wu Zhifan of the Qing Dynasty; height 15 cm, mouth diameter 8.5 cm, bottom diameter 8.7 cm. This holder is of fine quality bamboo, with a delicately carved design based on a Chinese folk legend, "Liu Hai Plays with a Golden Toad." According to the legend, the golden toad was a spirit which brought wealth to anyone who acquired it. Liu Hai was an immortal of the Five Dynasties, whose original name was Cao (some say it was Zhe). He became an immortal through studying Taoism and was styled Haichanzi (Sea Toad). People in later generations revered him as the god of happiness. Carved on one side of the holder is an image of Liu Hai, feet bare and wearing clothes with neck and shoulders exposed. With a beaming face, he sits cross-legged on a broom and bends down to play with a three-leg golden toad. On the other side of the holder is a four-line poem with seven characters to a line inscribed in intaglio, praising Liu Hai's optimism and his leisurely and carefree character. An inscription says that the design was carved by Wu Zhifan on the day before the Qingming Festival (tomb-sweeping day) in 1703, the 42nd year of Kangxi's reign. Wu Zhifan, a well-known artist in bamboo carving of the early Qing, was skilled in doing round sculpture and bas-relief. This holder is a masterpiece done in his late years.

247-1

248. Copper body enameled bowl with bat-and-lotus design   Decorative article of Qing; height 14.2 cm, rim diameter 31.7 cm, bottom diameter 19.8 cm. The process of making objects of this kind is first to make a copper body and then apply enamel glaze on the surface. The technique of making copper body enameled objects saw unprecedented progress during the Kangxi, Yongzheng and Qianlong reigns of the Qing Dynasty. The bowl shown here is decorated with a bat-and-lotus design, one of the traditional auspicious designs in China. The Chinese character for "bat" has the same pronunciation as the one for "happiness"; and the lotus, which emerges unstained from mud, is regarded as a noble plant. The Chinese character for it has the same pronunciation as the character for "unbroken." Thus the bat-and-lotus design implies unbroken happiness.

249. Brush with famille-rose porcelain stem and cloud-and-dragon design in gold tracery Stationery of Qing; length 24.8 cm. The porcelain stem is hollow; it is in famille-rose decoration with a cloud-and-dragon design in gold tracery. Fitted into the lower end of the stem is a tuft made of rabbit's hair. At the upper end is an inscription in seal characters that reads: "Made in the Qianlong reign of the Great Qing." The brush is one of the four treasures (brush, inkstick, paper and inkstone) of a Chinese study or studio. The technique of making these four treasures had reached a very high level in the Qing Dynasty. The best and most famous products were exquisite works of art, and some fetched very high prices at the time. Inksticks made by Chen Yiqing, a well-known manufacturer of inksticks, were extolled as "treasures as precious as gold."

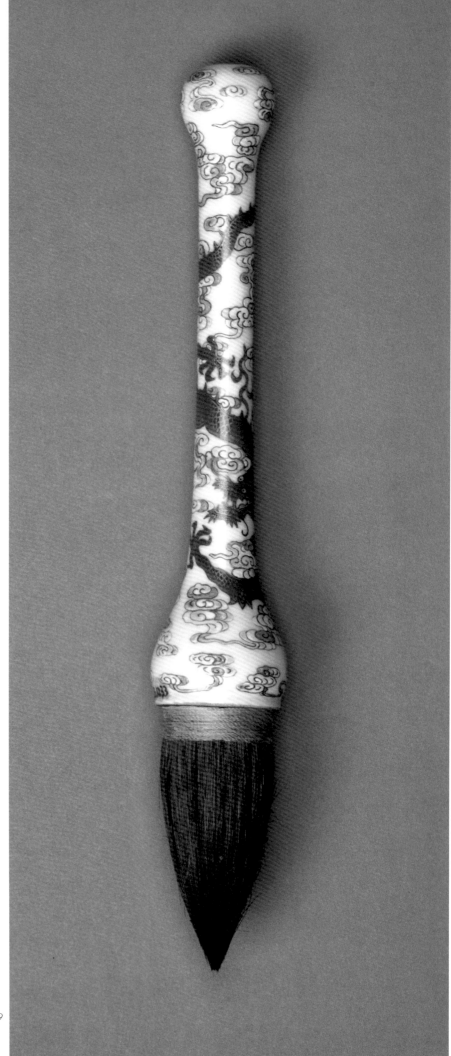

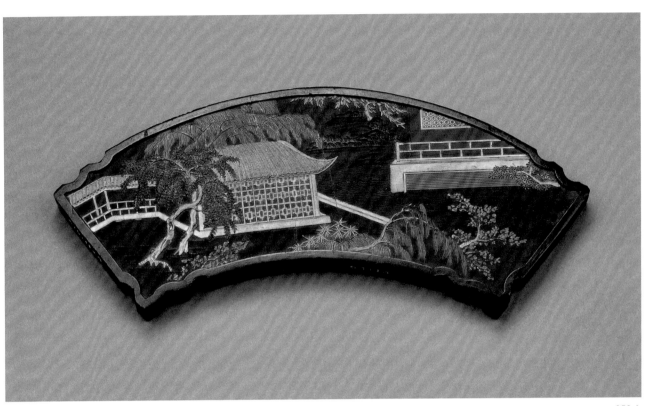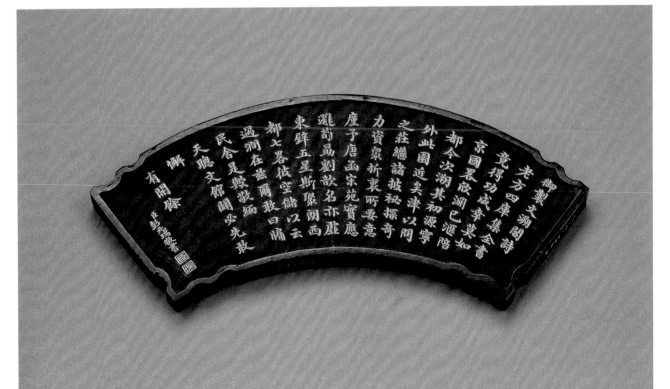

250. Inkstick used at Wensu Pavilion during Qianlong's reign Stationery of Qing; width of upper part 16.7 cm, height 5.5 cm, thickness 1.1 cm. The inkstick is shaped like a semi-annular jade pendant. On its obverse is a painted exterior view of Wensu Pavilion; on the reverse is a poem in regular script written by Emperor Qianlong. Wensu Pavilion, located in the western part of the Imperial Palace in present-day Shenyang, Liaoning Province, was one of the four treasuries in which *The Complete Library in Four Divisions* was stored.

250-1

250-2

251

251. Xuan paper with veiled design of two dragons playing with a pearl on a white background Stationery of Qing; length 64.1 cm, width 133.7 cm. Xuan paper is a high quality paper for writing or painting with Chinese brushes. It was first made in Xuanzhou (in today's Anhui Province), hence the name. The paper is white, soft, not easily worm-eaten, convenient for writing with Chinese brushes and can be stored for long periods. This kind of paper with veiled decoration was made by a special process.

252. Duan inkstone carved with peacocks Stationery of Qing; length 41 cm, width 33.4 cm, thickness 6.5 cm. The part for holding ink is flat but slightly concave. On the upper part is a carved design of a full moon, mountain rocks and pines with a pair of peacocks in their midst. Duan inkstone is a famous variety of inkstones. The stone is a product of Gaoyao County (in today's Guangdong Province). It is hard, smooth and dark purple in color.

252-1

252-2

253. New Year picture of a mid-autumn sacrificial ceremony

Qing relic, 60 x 102 cm. New Year pictures are a form of traditional Chinese painting; they are pasted on walls during the Chinese New Year. Most traditional New Year pictures are woodcuts with simple lines and bright colors and in a jubilant atmosphere. Records of woodcut New Year pictures date back to the Song Dynasty. In the Qing Dynasty, the most popular New Year pictures were made in Yangliuqing (now part of Tianjin), Taohuawu (in today's Suzhou, Jiangsu Province) and Wei County (in today's Shandong Province). The picture shown here depicts a sacrificial ceremony to the rabbit during the Midautumn Festival, which falls on the 15th day of the eighth month, mid-autumn by the lunar calendar. On the night of the festival, the moon is round and full, so the festival is also called a "festival of reunion." It is a Chinese traditional festival during which people have the custom of offering sacrifices to the rabbit. A Chinese myth goes that in the moon there is a rabbit pounding medicine in a mortar under a cassia tree, so people sometimes refer to the moon as a "rabbit wheel" or "jade rabbit," and offering sacrifices to the rabbit implies the offering of sacrifices to the moon. The Chinese name of the picture shown here is *Guixu Shengping* which translates literally as "The Cassia Is the Prelude to Peace." *Gui* (cassia) has the same pronunciation as "riches", so people regard the cassia tree as a symbol of wealth and rank. In folk legends, the cassia is also related to the jade rabbit and the moon. Thus the title cleverly implies family reunion, wealth and peace.

254. *Techniques of Jieziyuan Paintings*

Qing book on the art of painting. Jieziyuan (Mustard Seed Garden) was a villa owned by Li Yu, a celebrated dramatist of the Qing Dynasty. The book was compiled by Wang Gai at the request of his friend Shen Xinyou, Li Yu's son-in-law. Later, additions and deletions were made by the Wang brothers — Wang Gai, Wang Shi and Wang Nei. Wang Gai, styled Anjie, was a native of Xiushui (in today's Zhejiang Province) who lived in Jinling (today's Nanjing). He was good at doing large-size landscape paintings. Wang Shi, his elder brother, styled Micao, was well

254-1

254-2

versed in painting flowers and birds.
Wang Nei, his younger brother, styled
Xizhi, was also a good painter. This book
was printed from woodblocks and is in
three volumes. Volume One is an
elementary introduction to ways of
learning painting; it tells how to paint
trees, rocks, human figures, houses and
temples. Volume Two shows how to paint
orchids, bamboos, plum blossoms and
chrysanthemums; and Volume Three
shows ways of painting grass, insects and
flowers. The book explains profound
theories in simple language that is brief
and to the point. It is an important
reference work designed as an aid to
beginners who wish to learn the art of
painting.

255. Hibiscus and Duck   Painting by Zhu
Da of the Qing Dynasty, 121 x 42 cm. Zhu
Da (1626-c.1705) was a descendant of the
Ming nobility. When he was 19 years old,
the Ming Dynasty was overthrown. After
the establishment of the Qing Dynasty, he
concealed his identity and, at 23, became
a Buddhist monk, using the name Zhu Da.
Later he returned to secular life. At 59, he
began using the name Bada Shanren which
thenceforth became known far and wide.
He swore that he would never cooperate
with the Qing court all his life. Unbending
and defiant, he often wrote poems and did
paintings and calligraphy to give vent to
his indignation and loneliness. In most of
his paintings, he expressed his feelings
through creatures like fish and birds,
which he depicted looking upon people
with disdain. His most notable
achievements are in flower-and-bird
paintings, which show strong
individuality. His landscape paintings are
mostly in ink and wash.

256. Orchids and Bamboos Painting by Zheng Xie of the Qing Dynasty, 134.3 x 75 cm. Zheng Xie (1693-1765), styled Kerou, also known as Zheng Banqiao, was a native of Xinghua (in today's Jiangsu Province). He was good at painting orchids, bamboos and rocks, especially bamboos in ink and wash. He formulated the theory of three stages in creative work: "bamboo in the eye," "bamboo in the mind" and "bamboo in the hand." He once said, "The orchids, bamboos and rocks I paint are for the working people, not for those who sit idly by and enjoy the fruits of others." His ink bamboos are depicted as forceful and tenacious, proud and aloof, straight and upright. They seem to be a reflection of his own character. He used dry and light ink, vigorous but thin brush strokes, and both sparse and dense spacing. He attached importance to the organic combination of poetry, calligraphy and painting. Sometimes he painted with calligraphic strokes. For instance, when doing orchid leaves, he used the perpendicular stroke and left down-stroke of the cursive script in Chinese calligraphy.

257. Hibiscus and Twin Egrets
Painting by Zou Yigui of the Qing Dynasty, 163.6 x 94 cm. Zou Yigui (1686-1772), styled Yuanbao, also called Xiaoshan, was a native of Wuxi (in today's Jiangsu Province). He was a celebrated painter of the Qing Dynasty who specialized in flowers and plants. When painting flowers and plants, he used strong colors for petals or applied light color washes. He had a bright and elegant style and his paintings were vivid and natural. In his book entitled *On the Art of Xiaoshan's Painting,* he expounded the techniques of painting flowers and birds, which had a strong influence on later generations. The painting shown here was done on paper and signed by the artist. On the upper left corner is a poem with seven characters to a line written by Emperor Qianlong. The painting was preserved in the Qing imperial palace.

Decline and Downfall of the Qing Dynasty

During the late Qing Dynasty, local officials were both corrupt and incompetent and the people were near destitute. Natural and man-made calamities befell one after another and peasant uprisings occurred all over the country, culminating in the great rebellion of the Taiping Heavenly Kingdom and the collapse of the last feudal regime. At the same time, Western powers launched wars of invasion against China and forced the Qing government to sign a series of unequal treaties, ceding territory, paying indemnities, and relinquishing sovereign rights. Carving up of China by imperialist powers reached a high tide after the Sino-Japanese War of 1894-1895. With the Qing government on the verge of collapse, bourgeois democratic ideology gradually developed and bourgeois revolutionary organizations and professional revolutionists such as Sun Yat-sen emerged. Armed struggles broke out in various parts of the country. On October 10, 1911, the Revolutionary Party launched the Wuchang Uprising and set up a revolutionary military government. Subsequently, local governments in various parts of the country proclaimed their independence. On January 1, 1912, a provisional government of the Republic of China was founded, which led to the overthrow of the Qing Dynasty and signaled the final withdrawal from the stage of history of feudal dynasties which had ruled China for more than two thousand years.

Decline of the Qing Dynasty

Toward the end of the Qing Dynasty, the imperial court had become extremely corrupt, making life for the common people increasingly difficult. People of all nationalities waged struggles against such corruption, and the Taiping Peasant Uprising severely shook the rule of the Qing court. At the same time, foreign powers launched a series of wars against China, such as the Opium War, the Second Opium War, the Sino-French War, the Sino-Japanese War and the invasion of the Eight- Power Allied Forces. China's sovereignty and territory were seriously encroached upon by a number of unequal treaties. After the Sino-Japanese War, imperialist powers leased land in China, set up banks and exported capital to China. By way of economic aggression, they exerted an ever greater influence over the Chinese government. China sank deeper and deeper into the abyss of semi-colonialism, as the Qing government tottered in the midst of domestic turmoil and foreign aggression.

259

258. Opium smoking set Utensils of the late Qing; height of lamp 10 cm, diameter7.6 cm; height of opium holder 4.8 cm, diameter 6.5 cm; height of opium case 3.4 cm, diameter 3.8 cm; length of pipe 60 cm. Britain's trade with China increased considerably after the mid-18th century. However, as China's self-sufficient natural economy spontaneously resisted the dumping of capitalist industrial products, it enjoyed a favorable trade balance with Britain year after year. In an effort to change the situation, the British government resorted to the vicious scheme of exporting opium to China. This opium trade cost China large quantities of silver and increased the economic burden on the Chinese people. Moreover, opium smoking poisoned the people both physically and mentally. The Qing government was confronted with the double calamity of a shortage of silver and an enfeebled army. Under these circumstances, Emperor Daoguang sent Lin Zexu, governor-general of Hunan and Hubei provinces, as an imperial commissioner to Guangdong to enforce a ban on opium. Lin publicly burned more than 20,000 chests of confiscated opium at the Humen beach. The British government, to protect its opium trade, launched the first Opium War against China in June 1840. Soon the Qing government had to compromise and surrender; it relieved Lin Zexu of his duties and placed him under investigation. In August 1842, representatives of the Qing government and Britain signed the Treaty of Nanjing, the first unequal treaty in Chinese history.

259. Hong Kong in its early days as a treaty port Oil painting of the late Qing, 89 x 57.5 cm. In 1830, British traders submitted a paper to the British Parliament,demanding occupation of a Chinese coastal island to protect their trade with China. Later, W. Jardine, an opium trader, advised H.J.T. Palmerston, the then British foreign secretary, to occupy Hong Kong. The British army quickly occupied HongKong during the Opium War, and in the Treaty of Nanjing signed in 1842, the Qing government ceded Hong Kong to Britain. Later, by the Sino-British Convention of Beijing, signed in October 1860, the Qing government was compelled to place a portion of Kowloon under the administration of Hong Kong. In 1898 Britain for ced the Qing government to issue a special regulation to extend the boundary line of Hong Kong, leasing the Kowloon Peninsula and the islands around it to Britain for a period of 99 years, until the year 1997, and thus expanding British ruled territory in the Hong Kong area. This oil painting shows Hong Kong when it was first opened as a trade port.

260

260. Macao Oil painting of the late Qing; 62.5 cm x 49 cm. The Portuguese were among the earliest Westerners to come to China. In 1557, they leased Macao by cheating and bribing the local officials. In the beginning China retained the right to administer Macao. The Portuguese had to pay rent and commercial taxes to the Chinese government, and when a Portuguese was involved in a lawsuit with a Chinese, the case was tried by Chinese officials. After the Opium War, Portugal gradually encroached upon China's sovereign rights in Macao. In 1849, it expelled all Chinese officials from Macao, stopped paying land rent and forcibly occupied the place. In March 1887 the Qing government signed a treaty with Portugal, allowing the Portuguese to remain in Macao indefinitely and to administer the city and the areas around it. Macao became a *de facto* ceded territory. The oil painting shows Macao during the late Qing.

261. Copper coins of the Taiping Heavenly Kingdom Coins minted by the Taiping Heavenly Kingdom during the late

Qing. In January 1851, Hong Xiuquan led the members of the "Society for the Worship of God" to stage an uprising at Jintian Village, Guiping County, Guangxi Province. He established the Taiping (Great Peace) Heavenly Kingdom and named himself Heavenly King. In September, after the Taiping army had conquered Yong'an, Guangxi Province, Hong Xiuquan established military and

political systems and gave titles to several leaders. Subsequently, the Taiping army left Guangxi and fought in Hunan and Hubei provinces. In March 1853 Nanjing was captured, its name was changed to Tianjing (Heavenly Capital), and it was made the capital of the Heavenly Kingdom. In the years that followed, the Taiping armies fought well and crushed two large enemy camps north and south

of the Yangtze River, which the Qing government had set up for the purpose of surrounding Tianjing. In 1856, however, internal dissension and rifts appeared within the leading clique of the Taiping Heavenly Kingdom, greatly weakening its strength. Under the joint attacks of foreign invaders and the Qing government, Tianjing fell in July 1864 and the Taiping Uprising was defeated. During the years immediately after Tianjing became the capital of the Heavenly Kingdom, various systems and measures were promulgated by the Taiping leadership. The Heavenly Land System, promulgated in the winter of 1853, was a very concrete program, with land problems as the nucleus but also involving politics, military affairs and the economy. The system outlined an ideal heavenly kingdom, in which land would be equally distributed according to the number of members of a family; it stipulated that everything should be shared equally, and that all under heaven should be well fed and well clad. However, it was difficult to carry out the system in practice. In the beginning, the system of all wealth going to the state treasury implemented during the uprising at Jintian Village was continued. All residents enjoyed the supply system — a system of payment in kind. But later, because of difficulties in maintaining it, the system had to be abandoned, and the system of buying and selling commodities restored. In 1854 the Taiping Heavenly Kingdom minted coins for circulation in the market, bringing prosperity to the nation's commerce for a time.

262-2

262. Extant volume from *The Complete Library in Four Divisions* stored in Wenyuan Pavilion of Yuanmingyuan Qing Dynasty. The volume shown here is a survivor of a holocaust. It has a deep red cover, and the last page is stamped with a seal, "Treasure of Yuanmingyuan" ("Garden of Perfect Splendor"), in which the Complete Library was stored. Located in the northwestern suburbs of Beijing, Yuanmingyuan was an imperial garden of the Qing Dynasty. It took over a hundred years to build the garden, which covered an area of 200 hectares. In the garden were more than 140 scenic spots, 100 bridges, and numerous towers, pavilions, halls and other buildings, with a total floor space of 160,000 square meters. The garden used to be called the "garden of gardens" and "paradise on earth." In 1860 British and French armies invaded Beijing, after looting the treasures housed in Yuanmingyuan, they set it on fire, razing it to the ground.

262-1

263. Portrait of Deng Shichang Deng Shichang (1849-1894), styled Zhengqing, was a native of Panyu (today's Guangzhou), Guangdong Province. He was the captain of the warship *Zhiyuan* of the Beiyang Fleet. When the Sino-Japanese War of 1894 broke out, the Beiyang Fleet engaged a Japanese fleet on the Yellow Sea in September the same year. Deng Shichang led the officers and soldiers of the *Zhiyuan* in a fierce fight against the enemy. When his ammunition ran out, he tried to ram his vessel against an enemy ship, determined to sink both ships. Unfortunately, his ship was hit by an enemy torpedo before it could reach the

263

Balfour, Britain's first consul in Shanghai, forced Gong Mojiu, the magistrate of Shanghai, to agree to the leasing of land north of Yangjinbang and south of Lijiachang to British traders, allowing them to build residences there. By November 1848, after being expanded several times, the leased land totaled 2,820 *mu* (one *mu* = 0.06 hectare). In June 1863, the American consul forced Wu Jianzhang, then magistrate of Shanghai, to delimit a tract of land (7,856 *mu*) on the north bank of the Suzhou River as an American settlement. In September the same year, the British and American settlements merged to become the Shanghai International Settlement. In the beginning, the Chinese government had the right to intervene in the administration and jurisdiction of the settlements, over which it still retained territorial sovereignty. But with the expansion of imperialist occupation in China, the rights that China had reserved were totally disregarded and settlements became "states within a state." The picture here shows a scene on Nanjing Road in the Shanghai International Settlement in the late Qing Dynasty.

265. Banknotes issued in China by foreign banks and circulated during the Late Qing Not long after the Opium War, the Western powers, in order to carry out their economic aggression, began to set up banks in China. Up to 1897, foreign banks monopolized China's banking. They lent money at exorbitant interest rates to

Chinese traders and the Qing government, engaged in political investment as well as investments in factories, mines and enterprises; built railways and carried out trade and other economic activities. Thus, foreign banks controlled China's finance, banking, trade, transportation, factories and mines. Taking advantage of the fact that China's financial institutions were not sound and credit systems were not well developed, foreign banks issued large amounts of banknotes for circulation in China, reaping huge profits and controlling China's financial market. They issued banknotes without being subject to the surveillance of the Chinese government; nor did they register what they issued. Such acts seriously violated the sovereign rights of China.

264

enemy. The brave captain and all his men (over 250) lost their lives. During the Sino-Japanese War, Chinese officers and soldiers fought heroically, but they failed because of ineffective command at the top and insufficient supplies. In the end, the Qing government had to send Li Hongzhang to negotiate peace with Japan at Shimonoseki. In April 1895, the humiliating Treaty of Shimonoseki was signed.

264. A scene on Nanjing Road in the former International Settlement in Shanghai After the Opium War, the Qing government opened many treaty ports. Parts of those ports were delimited as settlements under the jurisdiction of foreign powers, the British-American International Settlement in Shanghai being the earliest. In November 1845, G.

266

266. Beijing's Zhengyang Gate after being burnt by the Eight-Power Allied Forces Picture of the late Qing. After the Sino-Japanese War of 1894-1895, imperialist attempts to carve up China reached high tide. The Chinese people rose to save the nation, and their struggles led to the outbreak of the anti-imperialist and anti-aggression Yihetuan Movement (called the Boxer Uprising in the West). To suppress the movement, Britain, France, Germany, Japan, Russia, Italy, Austria and the U.S. sent troops to China in June 1900. They seized Tianjin and Beijing, and attacked the Shanhai Pass in the east, Baoding in the south, Zhangjiakou in the north and Niangzi Pass in the west. Under the pretext of searching for Yihetuan members, they burnt, killed and looted wherever they went. The picture shown here is a view of Beijing's Zhengyang Gate set on fire by the invaders.

Table of Major Unequal Treaties Signed in the Late Qing

Name of Treaty	Date	Main Terms
Sino-British Treaty of Nanjing	August 29,1842	1.China opens Guangzhou, Fuzhou, Xiamen, Ningbo and Shanghai as trade ports. 2.China cedes Hong Kong to Britain. 3.China pays Britain an indemnity of 21 million silver dollars. 4.Tariff on British goods are subject to negotiations between China and Britain.
Sino-British Treaty of Tianjin	June 26, 1858	1.China opens Niuzhuang, Dengzhou, Tainan, Chaozhao, Qiongzhou, Hankou, Jiujiang, Nanjing, Zhenjiang as trade ports. 2.British warships are allowed to sail into the trade ports. 3.Christian and Catholic missionaries are free to carry out missionary activities in China's interior. 4.China pays Britain an indemnity of 4 million taels of silver.
Sino-French Treaty of Tianjin	June 27, 1858	1.China opens Qiongzhou, Chaozhou, Tainan, Danshui, Dengzhou and Nanjing as trade ports. 2.French warships are allowed to sail into the trade ports. 3.Christian and Catholic missionaries are free to carry out missionary activities in China's interior. 4.China pays France an indemnity of 2 million taels of silver.
Sino-British Convention of Beijing	October 24,1860	1.China opens Tianjin as a trade port. 2.China cedes a part of Kowloon to Britain. 3.China pays Britain an indemnity of 8 million taels of silver.
Sino-French Convention of Beijing	October 25,1860	1.China opens Tianjin as a trade port. 2.China pays France an indemnity of 8 million taels of silver.
Sino-Japanese Treaty of Shimonoseki	April 17, 1895	1.China cedes to Japan Liaodong Peninsula, Penghu Islands, Taiwan and its adjacent islands. 2.China pays Japan an indemnity of 200 million taels of silver. 3.China opens Shashi, Chongqing, Suzhou and Hangzhou as trade ports; Japanese vessels are allowed to sail into these ports along China's inland rivers. 4.Japan is allowed to open factories in China's trade ports. 5.Japanese goods manufactured in China are exempt from taxation; Japan is allowed to set up warehouses in China's interior.
Treaty of 1901	September 7, 1901	1.China is to pay eleven countries (Britain, U.S., Russia, Germany, Austria, France, Italy, Japan, Belgium, Spain and Holland) an indemnity of 450 million taels of silver within 39 years. The unpaid balance carries an annual interest of 4 per cent. 2.Foreign countries are allowed to station troops in Beijing, and along the railway line between Beijing and Shanhai Pass; the fort at Dagu and all forts from Dagu to Beijing are dismantled. 3.A legation quarter is set up in Beijing's Dongjiaominxiang where foreign countries are allowed to station troops. 4.The Qing government is to inflict severe punishment on "chief offenders, including ministers," and forbids the Chinese people to set up or participate in anti-imperialist organizations; violaters are to be put to death.

Revolution of 1911 and the
Downfall of the Qing Dynasty

As imperialist aggression intensified, the Qing government became increasingly corrupt and helpless. Bourgeois democratic thinking gradually developed in China and bourgeois propagandists like Zhang Taiyan and revolutionists headed by Sun Yat-sen came to the fore. In 1905 the Chinese Revolutionary League was founded, which had the characteristics of a revolutionary party. Its program was to struggle against the Qing government in order to overthrow Manchu rule and establish a republic. On October 10, 1911, following the success of the Wuchang Uprising, a military government was established in Hubei Province. In its wake, provinces in south China one after another declared their independence. On January 1, 1912, representatives of these provinces supported Sun Yat-sen's establishment of a provisional government of the Republic of China in Nanjing, with Sun as interim president. On February 12, 1912, Qing emperor Puyi announced his abdication, ending the feudal monarchy that had ruled China for more than two thousand years. The 1911 Revolution opened a new era in Chinese history.

267. *The Zhejiang Tide, Soul of the Yellow Emperor, Book of Grievances*

These three publications propagating revolutionary ideas of driving out the Manchus were published by bourgeois thinkers of the late Qing. *The Zhejiang Tide* was a periodical founded in Tokyo in 1903 by Chinese students from Zhejiang Province. A total of 12 issues were published. The contents included editorials, reviews, theories and biographies, and covered politics, laws, economics, philosophy, education, military affairs, history, current affairs and major events. The author of the *Soul of the Yellow Emperor* claimed to be "one of the direct descendants of the Yellow Emperor." It was published in 1903 by the Eastern Continental Press in Shanghai. It contained extracts of anti-Qing revolutionary works from newspapers and periodicals published in the Qing Dynasty, such as "On National Subjugation," "On Hatred of the Manchus," "Significance of the Yihetuan Movement to the Chinese Nation," and "Annals of the Yellow Emperor." *Book of Grievances* was written by Zhang Taiyan, also named Zhang Binlin, a revolutionary thinker of the late Qing. First published in Suzhou in July 1900, it contained 50 articles. Additions were made in 1902, and a reprint was issued in 1904 in Japan. A summary of Zhang Taiyan's political and social thinking in his early years, the book had a great influence on contemporary thinkers.

268. Fighters of Huanghuagang Uprising

On April 27, 1911, the Chinese Revolutionary League launched an anti-Qing armed uprising in Guangzhou. A 130-member dare-to-die corps, organized and led by Huang Xing, attacked from four routes the office of the governor-general of Guangdong and Guangxi. Fierce fighting took place between the dare-to-die corps and office guards, and the governor-general, Zhang Minqi, was forced to flee. Subsequently, the corps attacked various strategic points in Guangzhou and

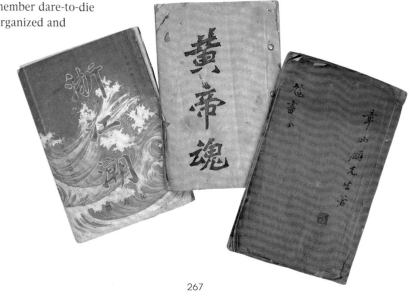

267

268

269

engaged in street fighting with the Qing army. After a whole day and night of bitter fighting, the outnumbered revolutionary fighters were overpowered with heavy losses; most were captured and died martyrs' deaths. The picture here shows the heroic, defiant fighters before their execution. Later 72 bodies of the martyrs were found and buried together at Honghuagang (later renamed Huanghuagang) in the suburbs of Guangzhou. The martyrs are honored in history as the 72 Martyrs of Huanghuagang. The uprising shook the whole country, and before long the Wuchang Uprising broke out. After the founding of the republic, the Huanghuagang Graveyard was expanded. A memorial archway, a grave-pavilion and a stone tablet were set up in 1918 with donations from overseas Chinese. On the memorial archway are four characters in Sun Yat-sen's handwriting, which read in translation, "Their noble spirit will never perish."

269. Attack by artillery troops of the revolutionary army in Hankou

On October 10, 1911, under the leadership of the Literary Association and the Society for Marching Together, revolutionaries in Wuchang took the lead in launching an anti-Qing armed uprising. At seven in the evening, Xiong Binkun, a revolutionary of the 8th engineering battalion of the New Army, led the uprising soldiers to occupy the Ordinance Bureau at Chuwangtai. Then other battalions occupied Phoenix Mountain and Snake Mountain and, in three routes, jointly attacked the office of the governor-general of Hunan and Hubei. The governor-general fled, and the revolutionary army took control of Wuchang. Following the victory of the first uprising in Wuchang, on the night of the 11th and the morning of the 12th units of the New Army stationed in Hanyang and Hankou also rose in rebellion. Soon the three cities of Wuhan (Wuchang, Hanyang and Hankou) were entirely in the hands of the revolutionaries. Yuan Shikai, a cabinet minister in the Qing government, amassed forces of the Beiyang Warlord Army and fiercely attacked the revolutionary forces in Hankou. The picture here shows artillerymen of the revolutionary army in Hankou firing at the Beiyang Warlord Army. Eventually, because it was not strong enough militarily, the revolutionary army retreated to Hanyang. On November 27, the Beiyang Warlord Army captured Hanyang, and Wuchang

270

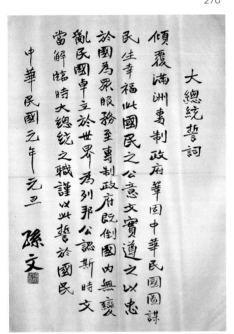

271

the third city was in a precarious situation. Yuan Shikai, however, was not disposed to take Wuchang immediately; he wanted to use the situation to bargain with the Qing government. Thus a confrontation rose between the north and south.

270. Portrait of Sun Yat-sen

Sun Yat-sen (1866-1925), also known as Sun Zhongshan and Sun Wen, was a native of Xiangshan (today's Zhongshan), Guangdong Province. In 1897 when he was in Japan, he used an assumed name, Zhongshan Qiao, hence he was generally called Zhongshan. In his early years he studied in his native place, but when still young went to Hong Kong to study medicine. Later he practised medicine and at the same time engaged in political activities. In 1894, while in Honolulu, he

set up the Society for the Revival of China — the first anti-Qing organization — and carried out anti-Qing activities. In 1905 he founded the Chinese Revolutionary League and began preparing anti-Qing armed uprisings. In the years that followed, several armed uprisings he led directly or indirectly ended in failure, but he did not lose heart and persevered in revolutionary activities in other parts of the world. Toward the end of 1911, after hearing of the success of the Wuchang Uprising, he immediately returned to China from abroad. Thanks to his high prestige, he was elected Provisional President of the Republic of China, and on New Year's Day of 1912 took the oath of office. After the fruits of victory of the 1911 Revolution were usurped by Yuan Shikai, Sun Yat-sen continued to fight to safeguard the Republic, initiating the Second Revolution, the Movement to Protect the Constitution and the Movement to Safeguard the Republic. Subsequently, he set up a revolutionary base in Guangzhou where the Huangpu (Whampoa) Military Academy was established and preparations for a northern expedition were made. After a coup d'etat in Beijing at the end of 1924, Sun Yat-sen went north to discuss state affairs with Feng Yuxiang at the latter's invitation. On March 12, 1925, he died in Beijing of illness caused by overwork.

271. Oath made by the Provisional President

Length 75 cm, width 45 cm. At the end of 1911, after the success of the Wuchang Uprising, provinces in south China all proclaimed their independence. Representatives from these provinces gathered in Shanghai and Nanjing to make preparations for a provisional government of the Republic. They supported Sun Yat-sen and elected him Provisional President. On January 1, 1912, Sun Yat-sen solemnly took the oath of office, the full text of which is reprinted here. It is in his own handwriting, and reads: "To overthrow the Manchu autocratic government, to consolidate the Republic of China, and to make efforts to improve the people's livelihood are the will of the people. I, Sun Wen, will carry out these tasks in loyalty to the country and in order to serve the masses. When the autocratic government is overthrown and there are no more disturbances, when the Republic stands strong and steady and is recognized by countries worldwide, I will relieve myself of the duties of provisional president. This is my pledge to my people."

272

272. First National Assembly of the Chinese Republic   After taking the oath of office as Provisional President, Sun Yat-sen released his inaugural address and telegraphed all provinces to abolish the lunar calendar and adopt the Gregorian calendar, stating that January 1, 1912 marked the beginning of the republic. On January 3, Sun Yat-sen presided over a national assembly, at which a list of his nominations for high-ranking officials and officers was adopted. It included the chiefs and deputy chiefs of the general staffs of the army and navy, and ministers and vice ministers of foreign affairs, justice, finance, internal affairs, education, industry and commerce, and communications. Provincial representatives elected Li Yuanhong Vice-President of the Republic. This was a coalition government of revolutionaries, constitutionalists and old bureaucrat politicians. According to the plan that "ministers were in name and vice ministers in reality," the real power of the government was basically in the hands of members of the Chinese Revolutionary League. The picture here shows the site of the national assembly. On January 5, 1912, members of a newly established cabinet held its first meeting on state affairs in the Presidential Palace. The Provisional Central Government of the Republic of China was thereby founded.

273

273. Senate of the Provisional Government of the Chinese Republic
On January 28, 1912, soon after the establishment of the Provisional Government in Nanjing, representatives (three from each province) sent by provincial governors met in Nanjing to set up a provisional senate, the highest legislative body of the provisional government of the Chinese Republic. Sun Yat-sen and Huang Xing attended the ceremony. Lin Sen was elected Speaker and Wang Zhengting Deputy-Speaker to exercise parliamentary power. 38 other parliamentary members were elected, including Yang Rudong and Chen Taoyi

(there were some changes in personnel later). Under pressure from reactionary forces inside and outside of the country, the revolutionists compromised and on January 15 agreed to hand over political power to Yuan Shikai on condition that the Qing emperor abdicate and Yuan support the Republic. On February 12, 1912, Emperor Puyi abdicated, and the next day Sun Yat-sen resigned as Provisional President. On February 15, the Senate approved his resignation and elected Yuan Shikai to replace him. On February 20, it elected Li Yuanhong as vice-president. Between February 7 and March 8, the Senate formulated and adopted the Provisional Constitution of

the Chinese Republic, which specified the state system and form of government, the rights and duties of the people, and the political system of separation of executive, legislative and judicial powers. It possessed the characteristics of a bourgeois republican constitution. The Constitution limited the power of the president. After taking over the post of president, Yuan Shikai refused to set up his office in Nanjing. The Senate therefore moved to Beijing along with the Provisional Government. At the end of 1913, it was dissolved by Yuan Shikai. The picture here is an exterior view of the Senate House in Nanjing.

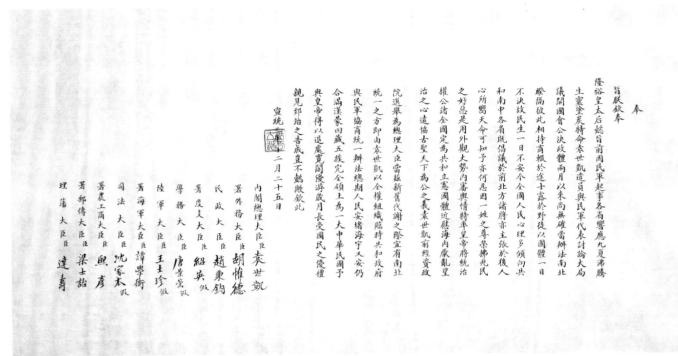

274-1

274. Imperial edict on the abdication of the Qing emperor and extra issue of *Capital Bulletin*

Length of imperial edict 75 cm, width 30 cm; length of extra issue 45 cm, width 35 cm. Under the coercion of Yuan Shikai, the Qing royal family issued on Feb. 12, 1912, an imperial edict announcing its abdication. It reads: "This is an edict from the Empress Dowager Longyu. Owing to the uprisings staged by the revolutionary army supported by various provinces, the whole country is in chaos and the people are suffering from extreme privation. I have ordered Yuan Shikai to appoint deputies to meet with representatives of the revolutionary army to discuss the situation and the convening of a national assembly and to decide by majority vote the system of government to be established. Now two months have passed and no proper way to solve the problems has yet been found. The north and the south are against each other, and neither side is willing to yield.... Today most people in the country favor a republic; provinces in south and central China have proposed the establishment of a republic; and generals in the north also support the proposal. It is the common aspiration of the people and the mandate of heaven.... So taking into consideration the current situation and the people's wishes, I have directed the emperor to transfer government power to the entire nation under a republican constitutional system.... Yuan Shikai was elected prime minister by a nominated advisory council. At a time when the new is to replace the old, it is necessary to have a plan for unifying the north and south. He has been given full power to discuss this with the revolutionary army to find a way to form a provisional republican government...." On the following day the *Capital Bulletin* carried the edict and issued an extra. Thus the feudal imperial system left forever the stage of Chinese history.

274-2

A Chronological Table

1271	Kublai the Mongol khan changes the name of his regime to Yuan and in the following year moves his capital to Dadu (now Beijing).
1279	Yuan conquers the Southern Song, unifying the whole of China.
1351	Red Turban army led by Liu Futong rebels at Yingchuan.
1368	Zhu Yuanzhang proclaims himself emperor in Nanjing and establishes the Ming Dynasty; he titles his reign Hongwu. The Yuan Dynasty is overthrown.
1376	The Zhongshu Sheng (Council of Ministers) at the central level is replaced by the Chengxuan Administrative Commissioner's Office; the whole country is divided into 13 administrative commissioner's offices.
1380	Prime minister system is abolished; the six ministries are responsible directly to the emperor. The Grand General Commander's Office is replaced by the Five Military Commanders' Office. Centralized power is strengthened.
1381	Yellow registers are compiled for counties throughout the country.
1387	Cultivated land all over the country is surveyed; results are compiled into the Fish Scale Illustrated Register.
1397	*The Codes of the Great Ming* is promulgated.
1402	Zhu Di, Prince of Yan, ascends the throne in Nanjing.

1405	Zheng He makes his first voyage to the "Western Oceans."
1409	The Nurkan Commissioner's Office is set up.
1421	The Ming court moves its capital to Beijing; Nanjing becomes auxiliary capital.
1436	Henceforth grain taxes in areas south of the Yangtze River are to be paid in silver instead of in kind.
1529	Ming government revises the system of having craftsmen in other parts of the country serve by turns in the capital; such service may be exempted on payment of silver.
1553	Portuguese colonists lease Macao by force.
1564	Japanese pirates along the southeastern coast of China are basically wiped out.
1573	Zhang Juzheng takes up the post of head of the inner chancery and begins to measure cultivated land across the country. He adopts a single payment system of taxation and carries out political reform.
1592	Japanese army led by Toyotomi Hideyoshi invades Korea. Ming government sends Li Rusong and others with troops to assist Korea.
1616	Nurhachi sets up the Later Jin regime in Hetuala.
1624	Dutch colonists occupy Taiwan.
1627	Wang Er leads an uprising in Baishui County, Shaanxi Province, marking the beginning of peasant uprisings in the late Ming.
1628	Zhang Xianzhong rebels at Mizhi.
1629	Li Zicheng rebels at Jin County, Gansu Province.
1636	Huangtaiji changes the name of his regime from Jin to Qing, and the name of his tribe from Nuzhen to Manchu.
1644	Li Zicheng establishes the Dashun regime in Xi'an and titles his reign Yongchang. Zhang Xianzhong sets up the Daxi regime in Chengdu, Sichuan Province, with the reign title Dashun. Li Zicheng enters Beijing in March; the Ming Dynasty is overthrown. The Qing Dynasty moves its capital from Shenyang to Beijing.
1662	Zheng Chenggong leads troops to Taiwan and drives out the Dutch; Taiwan is recovered.
1681	The revolt of three feudatories is quelled.
1683	The Qing Dynasty unifies Taiwan and in the following year sets up the Taiwan Prefecture under the jurisdiction of Fujian Province. Ban on maritime trade with foreign countries is lifted.
1689	Signing of the Treaty of Nibuchu (Nerchinsk) between China and Russia.
1713	Qing government announces that tax will not be increased for anyone born after the 50th year of Kangxi's reign.

1729	The system of combining land rent and labor levy is implemented in most parts of the country. The Qing government sets up a Ministry of Defense.
1755	Qing army marches into Ili; suppresses the rebellion led by Dawaqi of the Junggar tribe.
1757	Qing government suppresses the rebellion led by Amursana.
1762	Qing government appoints a general to govern Ili and strengthens its jurisdiction over the Xinjiang area.
1793	G. MaCartney, a British envoy, arrives in Beijing.
1821	Qing government orders a ban on opium.
March 1839	Lin Zexu, an imperial commissioner, is sent to Guangzhou to enforce the ban on opium.
June 1839	Burning of opium at the Humen beach.
June 1840	British navy arrives in the coastal area of Guangzhou; the First Opium War breaks out.
August 1842	Signing of the Sino-British Treaty of Nanjing.
January 1851	Hong Xiuquan leads the Jintian Uprising and establishes the Taiping Heavenly Kingdom.
March 1853	Taiping army occupies Nanjing, which is renamed Tianjing and becomes the capital of the Taiping Heavenly Kingdom.
October 1856	British troops attack Guangzhou; the Second Opium War breaks out.
June 1858	Treaty of Tianjin is signed between China and Russia, China and the U.S., China and Britain, and China and France.
October 1858	British-French allied forces invade Beijing; Yuanmingyuan is looted and burnt.
October 1860	Signing of the Convention of Beijing between China and Britain, and China and France.
April 1895	Signing of the Treaty of Shimonoseki between China and Japan.
September 1901	Signing of the Treaty of 1901
October 1911	Wuchang Uprising
December 1911	Revolutionary army occupies Nanjing. Sun Yat-sen is elected Provisional President of the Republic of China at a conference attended by representatives from 17 provinces.
January 1912	Sun Yat-sen is sworn in as Provisional President; proclaims the founding of the Republic of China.
February 1912	The Qing court issues an imperial edict announcing the abdication of the Qing emperor. Sun Yat-sen tenders his resignation as Provisional President to the Senate.
March 1912	Yuan Shikai becomes the Provisional President in Beijing.

A Brief Chronology of Chinese History

Palaeolithic Age			c.1.7 million—10,000 Y.B.P.
Lower Neolithic Age			c.10,000—5,000 Y.B.P.
Upper Neolithic Age			c.5,000—4,000 Y.B.P.
Xia			c.21st—16th century BC
Shang			c.16th—11th century BC
Western Zhou			c.11th century— 771 BC
Spring & Autumn			770—476 BC
Warring States			475—221 BC
Qin			221—206 BC
Western Han			206 BC—AD 8
Eastern Han			25— 220
Three Kingdoms 220-265		Wei	220— 265
		Shu	221— 263
		Wu	222—280
Western Jin			265—316
Eastern Jin			317—420
Northern & Southern Dynasties 420 - 589	Southern Dynasties 420 - 589	Song	420—479
		Qi	479—502
		Liang	502— 557
		Chen	557—589
	Northern Dynasties 386 - 581	Northern Wei	386—534
		Eastern Wei	534—550
		Western Wei	535—556
		Northern Qi	550— 577
		Northern Zhou	557—581
Sui			581—618
Tang			618—907
Five Dynasties			907—960
Liao			916—1125
Northern Song			960—1127
Southern Song			1127—1279
Western Xia			1038—1227
Jin			1115—1234
Yuan			1271—1368
Ming			1368—1644
Qing			1644—1911

Postscript

A Journey Into China's Antiquity is an art book based on the Exhibition of Chinese History on permanent display in the National Museum of Chinese History. More than three years have passed since the project for publishing such a book was first conceived. As the fourth and final volume goes to press, we would like to express our thanks to the Morning Glory Publishers, who conceived the project, planned and implemented it. At the same time, we are also indebted to the experts and scholars who over the years thoroughly studied the exhibition and made valuable contributions, and to many others who took part in improving and updating the contents. Besides the editors of the book and the text writers and photographers, all of whom are to be commended for their fine work, we must also mention Wang Hongjun, Du Yongzhen, Hong Tingyan, Chen Ruide, Ji Sen, He Qiyao, Song Zhaolin, Li Jiafang, Shi Guangming, Zhang Wanzhong, Shi Xuan, Zhang Zhenxin, Sun Guozhang, Fu Bin, Liang Feng, Wang Quanzhong and Chen Jishi, who participated in the overall planning of the exhibition, helped to make revisions, or prepared the maps and drawings. Li Ji also helped in the work. Our thanks are also due to Zhang Zhihua, Wang Yi, Guan Shuangxi and Ma Xiuyin, who during the compilation of this book coordinated the work of the many parties to the project, and to members of our own art department and storeroom who actively assisted in the project from beginning to end.

In short, *A Journey Into China's Antiquity* is the product of the joint efforts of the above-mentioned and a crystallization of their cooperation. Through its pages, may the myths, secrets and wonders of ancient Chinese civilization be revealed to readers around the world.

DU YAOXI

Deputy-curator

National Museum of Chinese History

October 1997